Teaching Talk

Teaching Talk

Strategies for production and assessment

Anne Anderson
Gillian Brown
Richard Shillcock
George Yule

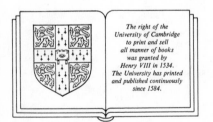

The right of the
University of Cambridge
to print and sell
all manner of books
was granted by
Henry VIII in 1534.
The University has printed
and published continuously
since 1584.

Cambridge University Press

Cambridge

London   New York   New Rochelle

Melbourne   Sydney

Published by the Press Syndicate of the University of Cambridge
The Pitt Building, Trumpington Street, Cambridge CB2 1RP
32 East 57th Street, New York, NY 10022, USA
296 Beaconsfield Parade, Middle Park, Melbourne 3206, Australia

First published 1984

Printed in Great Britain at the University Press, Cambridge

Library of Congress catalogue card number: 84–5013

British Library cataloguing in publication data
Teaching talk
1. Oral communication – Study and teaching (Secondary)
I. Brown, Gillian
001.54′2′0712   P95.3
ISBN 0 521 26528 2 hard covers
ISBN 0 521 31942 0 paperback

DS

Contents

Acknowledgments

We acknowledge the support of the Scottish Education Department for the project 'Competence in Spoken English'. The work reported in this book derives largely from that project. The opinions expressed are those of the authors, which do not necessarily conform with those of the Scottish Education Department. We acknowledge also the help of the Lothian Region Education Department in allowing us access to schools. A great many people have contributed in different ways to this book. We are particularly grateful to Sally Brown, Joe Casciani, Jeff Dodds, Richard Ellis, K.A. Hyslop, Marion Law, Cameron McMillan, Colin Peacock, Nigel Shadbolt, Hilary Smith, Stewart Smith, Stan Stephen, John Young, members of our Advisory Committee and to the staff and pupils of many Scottish secondary schools as well as to individual teachers, too numerous to mention. None of them necessarily agrees with everything we say here.

Introduction

A book written for teachers by people engaged in research sets itself up as a target for charges of 'ivory-tower mentality' and failure to recognise the problems of working in a classroom, with large numbers of pupils only a few of whom are motivated to work. Much of it may seem dry, over-technical, too theoretical, lacking in obvious applications.

In spite of these dangers, we persist in offering this book as a record of the outcome of research which, we believe, has relevance to any teacher who is concerned with the development of a curriculum in spoken language production.

One of the fundamental problems in the development of any curriculum, but perhaps particularly in a language curriculum, is the problem of principled grading, of setting easier tasks before more difficult ones, so that the pupil masters a particular skill and can be demonstrated to have mastered it in a range of new applications, and so that he can then go on to build on that foundation. In this book we are concerned with specifying how a spoken language curriculum can be developed which rests on secure principles of grading. Our discussion is concerned with what pupils find easiest to do well and the circumstances which help them to perform as well as possible.

Our hope is to offer the teacher a description of some of the variables which, we have found, affect a pupil's performance in spoken language, to show how a pupil's performance may be diagnostically assessed and so how the teacher can help the pupil to improve his performance. The work we have done results from analysing the performances of a large number of pupils, using spoken language to achieve a wide variety of ends. A good deal of our work has been in the form of descriptions of the language produced in controlled experimental settings.

Where the outcome of such research appears to have important educational implications, we have included a good deal of detail of the experimental methodology in the text. However the technical accounts, together with the statistical analyses of results, have been kept out of the main body of the text and included in Appendix C. We hope in this way to achieve a compromise between boring the reader who is not familiar with reading technical descriptions and, on the other hand, convincing the sceptical reader that our arguments are based on careful investigation and observation rather than on simple intuition.

We offer examples of a wide range of activities within a 'task-based' approach. In describing any particular task, we are merely exemplifying one possibility among a host of others. In Appendix A, we outline a range of further tasks which we have used with pupils, together with a brief discussion of what sort of language such tasks can be used to elicit – what sort of language use they offer practice in. We identify which tasks produce language which can be objectively assessed. In Appendix B, we illustrate a range of assessment protocols for task types discussed in the text. In each case we are concerned to show that, once the teacher has considered what sort of language a particular task demands of the pupil, he can use the types of diagnostic assessment which we illustrate here to see whether the pupil has any difficulty producing this type of language and, if he has, whether the teacher can help him to improve his performance.

Our main concern in this book is a limited one. We want to show that pupils' ability to use spoken language can, in general, be improved and to show in detail how this can be done. What we do not attempt is to make any suggestions about how the teacher should incorporate the particular aspect of a spoken language curriculum which we discuss here into a more general curriculum. This is because it seems clear that we are not addressing teachers in only one subject area. Whereas it may be the primary responsibility of English teachers to develop pupils' spoken language skills, teachers in other subject areas may equally require that pupils should be able to talk clearly and helpfully. 'Talking across the curriculum' seems just as appropriate a view to take as 'writing across the curriculum'. We don't suggest that in any subject, even in English, complete lessons be devoted to the sorts of practice we describe in this book. That would clearly be inappropriate and pupils would quickly become very bored. We suggest rather that pupils might be paired off, or organised into small groups, to undertake the sorts of exercises which we describe for 10 – 15 minutes a week.

The range of exercises which can be developed on the basis of the types of analysis we offer here is limited only by the time available to the teacher to develop more. It is worth noting that pupils rapidly become adept at developing their own tasks. Moreover pupils of 14 or so are quite capable of using the types of assessment procedures which we illustrate on tape recordings of their own speech. It may well be that this kind of self-assessment, undertaken either individually or in small groups, provides a really valuable opportunity for the pupil to take a hand in his own educational progress.

The pupils we have worked with have been 14–17 year-olds at Scottish secondary schools, in all cases native speakers of English. We should point out that although we have worked with Scottish pupils, the results of our work are not of exclusive interest to teachers in Scotland, but are relevant to teachers everywhere. The language which we illustrate frequently contains typically Scottish forms – forms like 'looks out his window' where Standard English would have 'looks out of his window' or 'greeting her eyes out' where Standard English would have 'crying her eyes out'. We have transcribed the speech illustrated here from tape recordings made during visits to many different schools. The transcriptions will look very disjointed to readers who are not accustomed to studying the detail of spoken language. It is worth noting that when a speaker is speaking about something which he feels confident about, he may speak more fluently than when he is rather uncertain or he finds what he is saying difficult to express. This is true of all of us, adult speakers as well as the teenage speakers whose speech we illustrate here. If you doubt this, try recording a conversation which you take part in and then make a careful transcription of what you've said – note the false starts, odd bits of messy grammar, and the minor hesitations (which we indicate in our transcriptions by +) and the longer pauses (which we indicate with + +). Note also the helpful and supportive noises made by listeners (which we represent in brackets as (hm), (uhuh), etc.).

We have been particularly interested in the talk produced by those pupils who are identified within the educational system as relatively unsuccessful in an academic sense. These are pupils who will, in general, leave school without any academic qualifications (under the current Scottish system of assessment, soon to be modified). They represent about 30% of the school population. We have concentrated on this population because the Scottish Education Department is in the process of implementing a recommendation made in the Munn Report (1977) that 'essential activities like . . . oral work in English' should not only be included in the curriculum but should also be assessed.

We have also worked with pupils who are identified as very successful within the educational system, who will proceed to take 8–10 Scottish 'O' Grades and who are, in general, expected to proceed to higher education. We should make it clear first of all, that judgments of relative academic success are made within the educational system, by a particular school, and that we work on the basis of that judgment and, secondly, that we have made no attempt to control for social class. We have made an intuitive appeal to the notion of social class in just one exemplary study: we recorded the voices of some academically able pupils who, we judged, had 'middle class' accents and some less academically able pupils who, we judged, had 'working class' accents and demonstrated that teachers ranked the pupils with middle class accents above those with working class accents except when they were asked to work with an objective scoring protocol when, in judging a particular skill, the pupils with working class accents were now ranked above those with middle class accents. (This study is described in Chapter 5, simply in terms of 'academically able' versus 'less academically able' pupils.)

The book is organised in the following way. The first chapter is about different uses of spoken language, which uses of language children seem to be naturally competent at, and what the school might usefully attempt to teach. The second chapter confronts some of the knotty issues related to dialect variation and class differences and asserts the neutral, non-interventionist, position which we adopt in this work. The third chapter outlines some of the general features which contribute to making it easier or more difficult for a speaker to feel comfortable in talking and explains in general the methodology which we have adopted. The fourth chapter works in detail through a range of task types, exemplified by specific tasks, and shows how different tasks make different demands on the speaker's ability to control the use of language. The fifth chapter shows in detail the assessment procedures which the teacher can use to diagnose where a pupil is having a problem. The sixth chapter suggests some of the ways in which a teacher can help a pupil to overcome a specific problem.

One final stylistic comment: we are of course aware that there are at least as many women teachers and girl pupils as there are men teachers and boy pupils, nonetheless we persist in using the traditional neutral forms 'he', 'him' and 'his' to refer to generic teachers and pupils, in order to avoid the constant repetition of forms like 'he or she' and 's/he'.

1 The spoken language

1.1 The spoken language in education

It is only relatively recently that educationalists have seriously considered that it might be necessary to teach the spoken language to native speakers of that language. For many years it was assumed that native English speaking children would naturally acquire the spoken form of the language. Since it is demonstrable that normal children at five, or ten or fifteen do indeed speak English and do show progressively greater command of English as they grow older, it seems reasonable to suppose that if they're simply left to grow up in an English-speaking environment they will naturally acquire competence in using the spoken language. If they are going to acquire spoken English naturally, over a normal period of development, there seems little point in applying scarce educational resources to what doesn't, after all, seem to be a problem.

Set against this cheerful assumption of normal development which can safely be left to get on by itself, there have been increasing rumblings of unease. People concerned with the role of language in education have pointed out that not all children acquire the sort of spoken language which is highly valued within the educational system. Various views on the 'language deficit' of particular groups of children have been put forward. (Some of these are discussed in Chapter 2.) Teachers and educationalists have pointed out that 'extreme' varieties of accent and/or dialect may prejudice a child's chances of success at school. Surveys of employers (or potential employers), Social Security officials, and other administrators of a highly bureaucratised society have identified many expressions of concern at the inability of school-leavers to express themselves articulately. This concern has been manifested in efforts to 'upgrade' the spoken language production of groups of children judged to be particularly at risk, an increasing number of conferences and seminars on aspects of 'oracy', and a demand within the educational system that the spoken language should be taught and included within the school curriculum. The Bullock Report (1975), and the Munn and Dunning Reports in Scotland (1977) have all insisted that it is time to pay more attention to the explicit development of spoken language in schools. It is suggested that spoken language be both explicitly taught and assessed.

This implies that a child's command of spoken English is just as much the responsibility of the educational system as his command of the written form of the language. Just as, once he has 'learned to write' in the primary school, the child is not then abandoned to develop his writing skills by himself, so when a child has 'learned to talk', a process usually well in train by the time he enters primary school, he should not be left to get on with developing spoken skills by himself. Just as he needs explicit practice and guidance in developing competent writing skills, so he needs explicit practice and guidance in developing competent spoken skills.

It is sometimes the case, in spoken language as in written language, that a particular child may be given special help and encouragement by his parents in developing his ability to express himself. Some children appear to be peculiarly gifted in self-expression and develop rapidly, apparently without explicit tuition. The majority of children however, need help in spoken language just as they need help in written language, and just as syllabuses for the majority give help in development of control in writing, so help should be given in the development of control in speaking.

How are we to set about developing syllabuses for teaching control of spoken language skills? In order to do this, we need to have a clear idea of what we understand by 'spoken language skills'. The next sections will be devoted to some discussion of this initial problem.

1.2 'Chat': listener-related talk

Most of us spend a good deal of our everyday lives talking. Much of the talking we do is fairly undemanding. We chat to the postman or to the person standing behind in the bus queue. We chat to friends and colleagues at work as we arrive in the morning and during meal-breaks. We exchange opinions about the state of the weather, the traffic, the price of vegetables, the health of a mutual friend, the film on TV last night or some recent piece of national news. The ability to 'chat', to exchange amicable conversational turns with another speaker, forms the basis of social life. Our experience in this begins very early on. In the first weeks of a baby's life, the typical mother 'chats' to her baby, assigning 'turns' to it as though it were really participating in a conversation, a process which continues well into the period when the child begins to talk. Consider the mother's speech in the following extracts. The mother is talking to her two-year-old child:

(1a) well + we'll pretend we've made tea + you put the teacup down and
we'll go 'ksh ksh' + there's your cup of tea + you drink it nicely +
+ oh + is that nice + will Mummy drink her tea + + I'll drink my
tea + oh + it's a bit hot (blows into cup) blow on it + not mine –
yours + it's too hot + put it down again + put it down again + oh
you spilled it look at it + it's all over the place + have to mop it up
then

(1b) whoops + d'you want to give her some + + you give her that +
you're supposed to give her the saucer as well

Notice how the mother provides a comment on the 'turn' of the child as
well as her own turn, as she manufactures this 'conversation', which
might be reconstituted thus, if we specify the child's turn:

(2a) Mother: there's your cup of tea
Child: (takes cup)
Mother: you drink it nicely
Child: (pretends to drink)
Mother: oh + is that nice
Child: (assents)
Mother: will Mummy drink her tea
Child: (assents)
Mother: I'll drink my tea

(2b) Mother: d'you want to give her some
Child: (assents)
Mother: you give her that
Child: (gives)
Mother: you're supposed to give her the saucer as well

Young children in the early stages of acquiring language often play a
rather minimal part in the actual speaking of conversations. Adults talking to them seem, however, to be perfectly capable of including them in a
conversation, assigning to them all the 'turns' which the children don't
succeed in filling with speech. As the child develops, so typically, the
child fills more turns with speech. Most normal children will acquire language in these circumstances and will be 'socialised' into conversational
practice in this way, not only by parents but by grandparents, other adult
friends of the family, and, eventually, teachers at school. Gradually, too,
most children learn to interact verbally with siblings and peers. If any
aspect of talking comes naturally, it is surely this. In what sense might it
be said to be 'undemanding'? Well, someone you chat with is generally

someone you feel relatively easy, comfortable, with. And, in a chat, the topic of conversation is generally determined by the immediate interests of the participants and, if they get bored, they may move on to another more interesting topic. Furthermore, chats are not expected to have outcomes – the sole reason for chatting is that it oils the social wheels and we enjoy it. It is the sort of talk that we all do most often and it is the sort of talk that many of us do best.

Consider the following extract from a conversation between two women:

(3) A: I think this time we had such a potentially good team (uhuh) we really thought we had everything going for us + they proved whether they were good or not

B: they never were any good + the way they were playing

A: well I think each one of them is good in his own right but they're just not playing as a team and that's (uhuh) just what it amounts to

B: 'cos even in these smaller underdeveloped countries I think they play a lot as a team you know

A: I think so

B: and this is a good thing

A: I said last night + I got shouted at last night

B: well we'll see it while we're on our own

A: I said this country has got so many football teams (uhuh) and we're picking one out of this team (uhuh) and one out of that – a few different teams + + you shove them all in a pack and expect them to play together

B: for a couple of weeks

A: and + eh + in a couple of weeks (uhuh) and they just don't do it + + you get a country that's only got about three major teams (uhuh) and are used to playing together

B: of course + even if they took like erm a couple of a winger and a couple of mid-field players that were used to working with each other

A: yes + yes

B: from the same team or something

This extract is taken from a friendly, cheerful, highly co-operative conversation – 'chat'. It is clear that nothing in the world will change as a result of it. The two friends are just swapping opinions about what the world is like, talking for the sake of talking, passing the time together amicably in the way most of us spend much of our social lives. They have happened upon a topic which is currently newsworthy and which any sympathetic person can be expected to agree on, and they spend most of the interaction agreeing with each other – even though it's not always quite clear what they mean by what they say.

We have suggested that 'chat' forms the basis of normal social life. This is not to say that everyone is equally good at it. 'Chat' appears to form an integral part of the social skills of an individual and we are not all equally socially gifted. Some individuals may only have a comfortable chatting relationship with a rather limited set of people. Others appear to be perfectly at ease in chatting with almost anyone they meet, skillfully unearthing common topics of interest and sensitively judging when the other person wants to shift to another topic. (Still others, of course, like the Ancient Mariner, insist on chatting to any victim they can catch, relentlessly pursuing their own particular topics.) Attempts to teach or improve an individual's chatting or conversational skills only presently occur in a remedial context (e.g. speech therapy); many of the foundation skills in chatting are laid down in the pre-school years. 'Teaching chat' would be a very different project from the one we are proposing – it would be attempting to change things intimately connected with self-image/self-presentation. It is not at all obvious that this would be desirable as there is no pressure for it from educationalists or from the public at large, and we can speculate that the self-image might be very much more resilient than the skills/behaviour we are advocating changing; even if it were possible to translate the relevant theories of social skills into pedagogic terms, the 'teaching' would be different in kind to the teaching of the language which is used to transfer information which we shall go on to discuss in the next section.

1.3 Information-related talk

What we shall call 'information-related' talk is a necessary concomitant of most jobs and is the type of talk which dominates life in the classroom. Consider the following extract:

(4) Teacher: now + here we have a substance in which the heat is moving along the rod from a hot end to a cold end + + can anybody tell me the name we give to such a substance – a substance in which heat can flow + + nobody can tell me that + well + it's called a conductor + + anybody ever heard of that word before? + + good well + I'll put it on the blackboard for you + + it's called a conductor + + what we're going to do today is to have a look at some conductors

This type of talk, explicitly addressed to transferring information on a particular topic, is typical of a lot of classroom talk. Teachers talk on a particular topic, give instructions on a particular topic, ask questions about a particular topic. Pupils answer on that topic, consult with each other about it, or ask further questions about it.

Information-related talk is not exclusively found in the classroom. It forms part and parcel of many jobs. Job-related talk is found in many types of work place: policemen talk to witnesses in police stations, nurses and doctors talk in hospitals, driving instructors talk to learners in cars, foremen talk to workers in factories, master-plumbers talk to apprentices, travel agents talk to customers, hairdressers talk to travelling salesmen, 'front desk' personnel talk to clients in hundreds of organisations. The whole cumbersome organisation of bureaucracy rests on the ability of individuals to communicate with each other. Whereas much of this communication may be in writing, a great deal more is in the form of spoken language.

Information-related talk differs from social chat in that its purpose is primarily to transfer information to a listener who needs it for some purpose. Or it may be that the speaker needs the listener to have the information in order that the listener can respond in an appropriate way – by providing the appropriate treatment, giving him the appropriate form, telling him what he wants to know, and so on. The point of speaking at all is to have some effect on how the world is – to change things. It follows, then, that one of the requirements of information-related speech is that the message should be clear and clearly understood by the listener. It is often the case, in information-related speech, that speakers repeat themselves in different ways in order to try to ram home the message, as the teacher does in extract (4). Or speakers may repeat what a previous speaker has said, perhaps adding an extra piece of information as the teacher does in the following extract:

(5) Teacher: to use Pythagoras what do I have to have + + David + + I have to have a + + we use Pythagoras in a
    David: in a triangle
    Teacher: a right-angled triangle + + so I must now make a right-angled triangle and I do it in this way + and I call the right angle C + + how many sides do I need to know Debbie to be able to calculate AB?
    Debbie: two
    Teacher: two

Compare the careful and explicit repetition of this information-oriented language with the much less carefully structured language in the conversation on football cited in extract (3).

It is important not to suppose that we are suggesting that primarily listener-related language is somehow 'inadequate', compared with information-related language. On the contrary, we are suggesting that each of these major language functions demands different, appropriate, language. When the topic is what is primarily at issue, then it matters that the speaker makes his message very clear, transfers information efficiently, and checks that his listener has understood the message. When the listener is primarily at issue, then it matters that the speaker and listener feel comfortable with each other and are established as being friendly with each other. Any syllabus designed to develop spoken language skills should draw this distinction clearly, and make it clear that the language appropriate to one function may differ, in many important respects, from the language appropriate to another function. In designing a syllabus for 'teaching talk', it is important to understand that simply encouraging pupils to produce more of the listener-related speech which they are likely to produce anyway in their social lives, will not necessarily ensure that they develop competence in information-related language. Similarly, encouraging pupils to produce competent information transfer, will not guarantee that they will find it easy to establish and maintain comfortable social relationships by talking.

It is important not to suppose that we can draw an absolutely clear-cut distinction between primarily listener-related talk and primarily information-related talk. It's possible to characterise the ends of the scale (for instance an officer giving orders to a subordinate versus giggling 'chat' at a party) but distinguishing between them is often a matter of judgment. It is important, too, to notice that information-related talk often comes sandwiched between social chat, and that what starts as social chat may frequently turn into serious discussion. The reason for insisting on the distinction here is to draw attention to that aspect of using spoken language which pupils most often and most obviously have difficulty with.

1.4 What to teach

We have now interviewed more than 500 pupils in a range of Scottish secondary schools, pupils between 14 and 17 years old. The majority of these pupils (about 300) will leave school with no academic qualifications.* That is to say, they are pupils towards the bottom of the academic

*Relatively few Scottish pupils follow CSE curricula.

ability range as judged within the educational system. The remainder of the pupils are selected from those who are, at this point in their careers, judged to be academically successful, and will take eight or more Scottish 'O' Grades and are generally expected to proceed to higher education.

Taking our population as a whole, we found very few pupils who were not able to (or not prepared to) chat cheerfully and co-operatively with a visiting interviewer who they had never met before. Similarly, nearly all the pupils we worked with were apparently comfortable in co-operating with a second pupil in performing a task specified by the interviewer. That is to say, throughout this large population, we encountered fewer than ten pupils who appeared to be inhibited in participating in 'chat' – in using language to establish and maintain social relations. Naturally some individuals were less forthcoming than others but, in general, they seemed to be in control of basic social skills. They were able to answer questions, ask questions, check on their listener's state of knowledge, talk on a topic which they knew something about and introduce topics of their own. They could do all this under certain conditions, which we shall discuss in Chapter 3.

A rather different picture emerges when we consider the ability of these pupils to transfer information in speech. None of our population had any difficulty in passing on to someone else extremely simple information like:

(6) in the first picture + there's a boy +erm+ with a catapult + he's just turned round and he can see a + fly +flying about + and in the second picture +he's turned round again and he's still got his catapult in his hand + and there's a great big sunflower or something and the fly's heading straight for the middle of it

However, the majority of the population have considerable difficulty in describing, for instance, a car crash involving three cars which they have seen photographs of. It seems clear that transferring some types of information is a complex cognitive skill. With really difficult complex information to transfer, many pupils who were perfectly competent in 'chat' showed that they had considerable problems. The following pupil (P) has been reading *Jaws*, having seen the film twice. The interviewer (H) has said, on two different occasions, that she has neither read the book nor seen the film. The following conversation ensues:

(7) H: is the book like the film?
    P: + + a wee bit
    H: mmm + + what's different in the book?

P: in the book + + + Hooper dies in the film but he never dies but
    he went in a cage down + to see if he could see the fish + and like
    + + + and trying to get in + the fish + but he couldn't + + the
    fish turned er the cage over but then he went away and Hooper
    just went and swum out and hid behind a rock and + in the book
    he said that he died

To a listener who has no knowledge of book or film, this is very difficult
to understand. In the first line of the pupil's reply it is not clear whether it
is in the book or the film that 'Hooper' does or doesn't die. The listener is
not told who 'Hooper' is, or why he should be 'in a cage', or why he
wanted to see 'the fish'. It's not clear which 'he' 'went away', though the
reader may suppose it must have been 'the fish' since 'Hooper' then
swims out and hides. It's not clear who the 'he' in the last sentence is,
who said that 'he died'.

It is a noteworthy feature of this interview that the interviewer doesn't
check up, to sort out the unclarity, since, at this point, the interview is
supposed to be casual 'chat' to warm up the pupil before he is asked to
perform some tasks. This enables us to reiterate the point that, in casual
chat, the language used is often very imprecise – which seems to be perfectly appropriate and adequate where the purpose of the interaction is
'being friendly'. However in a situation where transfer of information is
at issue, where the point of interaction is that transfer, it must be clear
that this sort of unclarity is inadequate.

Since most pupils seem to perform adequately in primarily listener-
related speech but many perform inadequately in transferring information in at least some types of information-related speech, we believe they
should be explicitly taught to control the transfer of information in information-related speech.

If they are to be taught, then a syllabus must be devised. It is clear that
the syllabus should be structured, so that the pupils learn first to perform
relatively simple acts of information transfer, and only gradually move
towards the extremely demanding types of task which are illustrated in
later chapters. The main aim of this book is to discuss how such a graded
syllabus can be devised.

1.5 'Short turns' and 'long turns'

At the beginning of the chapter we illustrated extracts in which a mother
manufactured conversational 'turns' for her two-year-old. When the
child begins to take his own turns, they are characteristically short:

(8) Mother: that was yours + + do you want more
    Child: want more
    Mother: right + ksh + there you are + have some more + oh I think
             that's good + I think you're liking that
    Child: that's Mummy's
    Mother: yes – this is Mummy's + + Mummy's finished hers + + is
             Mummy to have some more
    Child: Mummy have s'more

It seems reasonable to suppose that it is easier for a speaker to plan and produce short turns than to plan and produce longer turns. Certainly in the population we have interviewed, all our subjects seemed perfectly competent in the planning and production of short turns (and, indeed in long turns in listener-related speech where control of information is not primarily at issue). It seems clear that one of the least demanding genres of adult conversation is the type where speakers exchange short turns in listener-related 'chat' as in the following extract:

(9) I: they're to pay the children to stay at school + + + better than
         going round to the dole at ten pounds a week
    K: it should be cheaper for the government
    I: yes + but that's dreadful isn't it
    K: it's a shocker
    I: I don't know what the country's coming to at all + where all the
         money's coming from + I don't know
    K: you'd think it would be better for them to pay them to do some-
         thing else + there's plenty needs to be done round about
    I: and look at the vacant jobs in the paper + it's amazing + pages
         and pages of vacant jobs and yet there's so many unemployed
    K: I know + it's amazing

This casual 'what's it all coming to' chat is typical of a good deal of unde-manding adult conversation. It's clear that I here is taking the responsi-bility for initiating in the main, and that K is taking a relatively passive role, simply responding to what I is saying. Even the longest turns only stretch to a couple of 'sentences' – and they generally involve a good deal of repetition. Not much information gets added at a time. Turns of this sort seem to be relatively easy to construct.

It is not possible to determine a 'cut-off' point between long and short turns. All we can say is the longer the turn, the more planning the speaker has to do. So a speaker who tells a joke, or an anecdote about 'coming to work/school this morning', or reports an accident to the police, or explains how a slide-rule works, has to do some planning and organise what he says in a way that is helpful for his listener. Whereas all speakers of a language seem to be able to operate quite well in short turns, this is by no means true of long turns. The control of long turns is something which very young speakers don't attempt and which young speakers in general (and some adult speakers) have considerable diffi-' culty with, especially when, for one reason or another, they are under 'communicative stress' (a concept to be discussed in Chapter 3). The problem with the young taking long turns is that they tend not to control the information flow very well – as we saw with the young speaker in extract (7). Adults in a hurry have a tendency to listen with half an ear to the outpouring or to try to stem it with an intervention. A young speaker trying to impart complex information needs a supportive and patient listener – not one who finishes off his sentences for him or keeps on interrupting, but one who listens with interest to what *he* has to say, even if it is banal and predictable, and he takes a long time to say it.

It seems reasonable to suppose that the ability to structure long turns in speech demands considerable skill and practice – just as the ability to structure long 'turns' in written language does. It must be clear that it is not sufficient for the young speaker simply to produce two minutes' worth of talk. We believe that simply practising listener-related 'chat' when information-transfer is what is at issue, does not necesarily improve your ability to transfer information. Long turns which are used to transfer information – to recount an anecdote, justify a position, give instructions about how to take some medicine, describe a route – demand skill in construction and practice in execution. In a relatively easy task – asked to describe how she gets to work, this young adult speaker performs extremely well:

(10a) well + in the winter time when I'm lazy + + I take a bus down to Morningside station which is all of about two hundred yards (laughs) + and then I get on + erm + a 23 bus at Morningside station + and it + goes direct to the Royal Botanic Gardens via + Tollcross + through the Mound + up Hanover Street + down into Canonmills + and into Inverleith Row

She speaks fluently and confidently as she recounts a daily routine where the language she uses is supported by the stable structure of the route. When asked to perform a much more difficult task, to justify the identification of a particular place in a photograph which she has been shown, she produces much less fluent speech:

(10b) this + that that + it looks like St Giles + now from which side it
       must be + it + no ah + I should think it's off the High Street
       somewhere + + + looking west towards St Giles + well + right +
       now well + it could be Chambers Street running off that way to –
       back to St Giles + you know + Chambers Street – yes + well + I'll
       say Chambers Street

The difficulty of the task is reflected in the language. It seems obvious
that, if we are to develop a syllabus for teaching control of long turns in
speech, we need to identify what are easy tasks and practise those first,
before moving on to complex tasks which even highly educated speakers,
like the speaker in (10b), have difficulty in performing fluently.

1.6 Written-language influenced speech

One of the characteristics of the speech of highly educated adults is that
the spoken language they produce may often closely resemble written
language. This is presumably explained by the fact that they have spent
so much of their time reading and writing in the process of becoming
educated and also because educated discussion is characteristically carried on in a kind of spoken language which is very like written language.
This is particularly the case when a speaker is rehearsing opinions which
he has expressed many times before. Much of the talk heard in discussion
programmes on radio and television is couched in language of this kind.
The formal characteristics of such language include using long, often
Latinate words, and using long, often complex, sentences. If the present
writers were having a discussion on the characteristics of spoken versus
written language, they would be very likely to produce in speech the sort
of sentence which you are reading now. Even teachers who are making a
very considerable effort to use simple vocabulary often produce quite
complex syntax as we saw in extract (5):

(5) . . . how many sides do I need to know Debbie to be able to calculate
       AB?

It is important to realise that spoken language heavily influenced by written language is typically produced by adult speakers who have spent a lot
of time being influenced by written language. This language is not
characteristic of young children and adolescents. It is true that we occasionally encounter highly academic adolescents who spend a lot of time
reading and writing and do produce surprisingly mature language, but it
must be clear that these are the exceptions. The spoken language produced

by the majority of young people, as indeed by the majority of the population, consists of relatively simple sentence structures – often just phrases and incomplete sentences, strung together, and rather simple vocabulary – words and phrases like 'got', 'nice', 'a lot of', 'thing', 'and so on'. Consider the following extract, spoken by a young (postgraduate) adult:

(11)   and + er + I was pretty exhausted and I phoned up room service and said that I wanted a sandwich + + nothing's ever straightforward in America (laugh) – 'what kind of sandwich' + + I said 'well' er + hummed and hawed + and he said 'well + there's a list in your drawer' + 'in your chest of drawers' + + so I had a look at it and gawd there was everything (laugh) you know + and I saw roast beef + so I phoned back and said I would have a roast beef sandwich (laugh) + and a glass of milk + so an hour later + + nothing happened you see + so I phoned him up again and yes + they were coming + and in walked this guy with a tray + an enormous tray and a steel covered + plate + dinner plate you see + so I lifted that up + and I've never seen anything like it + + there was three slices of bread lying on this plate + and there was I counted eight slices of roast beef + hot roast beef + with gravy and three scoops of mashed potato round the outside + an enormous glass of milk and a glass of water

This is told by a very competent story-teller, who structures long turns confidently. Notice the way clauses are strung together with 'and':

(11) . . . I was pretty exhausted and I phoned up room service and said that . . .

where in written language we might expect more structure as in:

. . . I was pretty exhausted so I phoned up room service to say that . . .

Notice too, the simple juxtaposition of clauses and phrases:

(11) . . . so an hour later + nothing happened you see + so I phoned him up again and yes + they were coming . . .

where in written language, again, we would expect more elaborate syntactic structure. Notice too that much of the vocabulary is very simple:

(11) . . . so I had a look at it and gawd there was everything you know . . . and in walked this guy with a tray . . .

Just as perfectly adequate listener-related chat can be couched in simple language so can information-related conversation. In Chapter 4, we exemplify the performance of a large number of speakers who produce perfectly adequate accounts using only rather simple language forms. It is important to realise that such normal spoken language forms are adequate for all the usual uses to which spoken language is put. It is not necessary to control complex spoken language in order to transfer information clearly. Indeed we would suggest that it is quite inappropriate to insist that adolescent speakers of a language should be taught to produce those forms which are characteristic of highly-educated middle-aged speakers of the language.

In this book, then, we are not concerned with a programme for teaching more forms of the language than a pupil already commands. We are concerned that he should learn to use the forms of language which he already has in an effective manner. This is the main difference between teaching pupils skills in structuring long information-related turns in spoken language and in written language. In many respects the skills required are very similar – in both cases information has to be selected, ordered and verbalised in a way that will be understood by a recipient who has specific requirements in terms of previous knowledge and present needs. However, in written language the pupil will need to learn some of the forms which are particularly characteristic of writing – the use, for instance, of forms like 'which' and 'therefore'. He will need, as well, to replace some of the typical spoken language forms by acceptable written forms – 'got' by 'have', perhaps and even 'a lot of' by 'much' or 'many'. In spoken language, the pupil does not need to learn new forms, simply to learn to use the forms which he already has in additional ways. It is hardly surprising that many teachers have pointed out that the development of teaching long information-related turns in spoken language may serve as a useful preliminary to teaching the same skills in written language.

1.7 Information-related long turns

We have argued for the relevance and importance of teaching control of the transfer of information in the spoken language. We regard this as a skill which pupils may not naturally acquire and which, therefore, needs to be explicitly taught. We emphasise again that we do not wish to claim that transferring information is the only, or even the most important, function of spoken language. We have argued, however, that it is the function which is in most urgent need of being taught.

2 Speech differences and social differences

Linguistics and psychology are the two disciplines underlying the theory contained in this book; the book itself is intended for the attention of teachers. There is always a danger involved in the import-export of terms and theories between disciplines; in the case of education and psychology, there are particular – not to say notorious – dangers. This chapter is intended to confront some of the more likely value-judgments and misunderstandings which accompany the subject of language and language use, to introduce a few useful perspectives from linguistics and psychology, and to show briefly some of the influences upon the approach described in this book. In many senses this chapter is a cautionary one, to be borne in mind whilst reading the rest of the book; suggestions are made at the end of the book for further reading which will amplify some of the topics mentioned.

2.1 Dialects and Standard English

It should be said at the outset that this book is only concerned with speakers whose native language is English. None of our subject population had learned English as a second language and the teaching of English as a foreign language does not fall under the remit of this book. (Readers are referred to G. Brown and G. Yule, *Teaching the Spoken Language*, Cambridge University Press, 1983, for a consideration of such issues.)

In discussing dialects, it is the relationship between the various 'varieties' of English which is at issue. In the studies reported in this book most of the pupils spoke various Scottish dialects; for instance, they would be more likely to say 'the car needs washed' than the Standard Southern English forms 'the car needs washing' or 'the car needs to be washed'. Similarly these speakers are equally likely to say 'what like is the weather?' rather than 'what is the weather like?', the latter being the one which is permissible for Standard Southern English speakers. Standard Southern English is simply one form of Standard English, the other forms including Standard American English, Standard Canadian English, Standard Scottish English, and so on. These are all equally legitimate standard forms.

The Scottish dialects spoken by the pupils in these studies, were all necessarily closest to Standard Scottish English than to any other standard form of English. These dialects depart from Standard Scottish English in varying degrees, in terms of minor vocabulary differences and differences in pronunciation, or accent. These dialect differences may be correlated with factors such as geography, social group, urban versus rural communities. A speaker of Standard Scottish English would normally refer to the hall and stairs serving a number of flats, as a 'close', for instance, but would be considerably less likely to use consistently the word 'bairn' to refer to a young child. When we look at Scottish dialects other than Standard Scottish English the word 'bairn' appears more commonly, and certainly appears in more dialects than does the expression 'ben the house' meaning 'through the house'.

Turning, for a moment, from differences between dialects to differences between languages, it is not the case that one language is any more complex, expressive, logical or advanced than any other language. Children learning their native language face a task of equal difficulty whatever the language. Once they have acquired it, they all possess a means of communication of the same complexity, creativity and expressive power; people in remote rain forests can acquire and deploy new vocabulary just as easily as people in Western cities, and their language is no less extensive and differentiated.

In just the same way, value-laden statements of the kind 'this dialect of English is more correct than that dialect' or 'this dialect is more expressive or logical than that dialect', are simply false. Languages change constantly. Words fall out of use and new ones enter the language. Words change their meaning; for instance, dictionaries may define the word 'decimate' as 'to kill one out of every ten', but it is now more commonly used to mean 'to kill nine out of every ten'. Languages change in things such as verb agreement; 'you were' has largely replaced 'you was', over the last couple of hundred years. The grammar of a language is likewise not immune to change. The spoken language is primary and any written forms secondary, so there can be no question of any prescriptivism which says that spoken language – as it exists at any one time – should not be allowed to 'degenerate' but should be forced to adhere to conventions captured in the written form.

At any one time a language varies across the parts of the population speaking that language. Just as comparisons between eighteenth-century English and nineteenth-century English are not made in terms of which one is the more expressive or the more 'correct', comparisons of that kind are not made with respect to different geographical dialects spoken by different parts of the population. All of this brings us to the simple position that Standard Scottish English and Standard Southern English are in no way prior or superior to any other dialect of English; it is an arbitrary historical fact that these particular dialects should have become the 'standard' dialects which are employed in school textbooks, in higher education, in the professions and the civil service.

This way of characterising dialects and dialect differences is not always clearly appreciated by many people working in education and by the public at large. As an example, it is widely felt that the Standard English form 'I never let anybody wash the car' is inherently more 'logical' than the non-Standard form 'I never let nobody wash the car'. There is a 'popular' view that, because the second one has a 'double negative' (or 'negative concord'), it means the precise opposite of the first one and that anyone using this second form is speaking badly and inadvertently saying the opposite of what they mean. The fact is that a speech community which uses the second form consistently is speaking just as logically as another speech community using the first form. Anglo-Saxon English used to possess negative concord, just as many present-day languages do – Russian, Spanish, French, Hungarian and Serbo-Croatian, for instance. The relation of Standard English to logic is one of convention: there is nothing inherently logical about the grammar of Standard English. Labov made this very point in 1973 in relation to the variety of English spoken by many black children in American schools. The following is an excerpt from a dialogue quoted by Labov; the speaker is a 15 year-old from Harlem, characterised by Labov as a 'paradigmatic speaker of non-standard Negro English (NNE) as opposed to standard English (SE)', and the conversation concerns life after death.

'Why? I'll tell you why. 'Cause, you see, doesn' nobody really know that it's a God, y'know, 'cause I mean I have seen black gods, pink gods, white gods, all color gods, and don't nobody know, know it's really a God. An' when they be sayin' if you good, you goin' t'heaven, tha's bullshit, 'cause you ain't goin' to no heaven, 'cause it ain't no heaven for you to go to.

The speaker frequently uses negative concord ('doesn' nobody really know . . . don't nobody know . . . you ain't goin' to no heaven'), together with several other forms of speech which depart from Standard American English; this speaker is nevertheless being quite consistent within his own speech community, and cannot be accused of speaking illogically.

Other examples could be given to demonstrate the fact that popular beliefs and intuitions about language and language use are often misconceived and misleading, and, when applied in a school setting, may act simply as vehicles for prejudice against dialect speech. A closely related issue is that of differences in language use which are associated with social class, which we now consider.

2.2 Language and social class

Since the late 1950s, sociolinguists have produced a body of work concerned with describing the language which is typically used by certain social groups and in certain social situations. Sociolinguists have investigated, for instance, the language used in situations involving authority, such as doctor-patient relationships, as opposed to the language used in talking within a peer group. More will be said on peer-talk in other parts of this book; for the moment, what is of interest is the claim that people produce different language depending on their socio-economic status.

Any discussion of this claim makes reference to Bernstein at some point. From 1958 onwards, Basil Bernstein wrote a series of articles claiming that there are two different varieties of language – 'public language' and 'formal language'; these terms quickly changed into the more well known 'restricted code' and 'elaborated code'. These two codes were defined fairly loosely. Restricted code was defined as language which was simpler, grammatically, having fewer subordinate clauses and tending to rely more on simple clauses joined by 'and'; it also contained fewer passive sentences. In contrast to elaborated code, it tended to rely more on relatively high-frequency (common) words; this means that children said to be using restricted code would produce relatively inexplicit expressions in order to refer to things, often just using a pronoun. Elaborated code was seen as a richer, more complex and less predictable type of language.

Bernstein claimed that all children had access to the restricted code, but that a child's access to the elaborated code was largely determined by social class. His later formulations of the theory have cast things in terms of the type of family responsible for the early socialisation of the child, the extent to which authority and control are exercised in that family, and the possibilities for the personal development of the child. Nevertheless, the most influential aspect of Bernstein's theory has been that part which associated lack of access to elaborated code with membership of working class or lower working class families, and access to elaborated code with membership of a middle class family. This theory was particularly attractive to educationalists looking for an explanation of the poorer school performance of lower working class children.

Bernstein's theories have received a considerable amount of criticism and, in response, his notion of the restricted/elaborated distinction seems to have moved away from the earlier very concrete, linguistic characterisations of two categories of language use, and towards more abstract definitions which are expressed as *tendencies* rather than as strictly defined categories.

The suggestions for further reading at the end of this book include lengthy critical appraisals of Bernstein's work; for the moment it is sufficient to remark that the distinction which Bernstein points to is very different from the type of distinctions which could be labelled as dialect differences. Controlled experiments – some of them reported in this book – have shown that very much more importance than Bernstein originally conceded, attaches to the context in which the language is produced; children who might previously have been labelled as having access only to restricted code have been shown to be capable of producing 'elaborated code language' under different experimental conditions or with different tasks. The minor grammatical and other differences which distinguish a dialect from Standard English are not sensitive to context in this way, nor is it the case that dialect differences are expressed in terms of the frequency of using such-and-such a form – a passive sentence, for instance; differences such as the ones recorded by Bernstein should perhaps be termed 'stylistic'.

Trudgill, in *Accent, dialect and the school* (1975), demonstrates the differences between the non-standard dialects and 'codes' in the following way:

According to Bernstein's list of 'code' features, a sentence such as
The blokes what was crossing the road got knocked down by a car
has characteristics of 'elaborated code' (a subordinate clause and a passive verb), whereas
The gentlemen were crossing the road and a car knocked them down
does not. The former, we can say, is non-standard dialect, with informal vocabulary, but 'elaborated code'; while the latter is standard dialect, with more formal vocabulary, but *not* 'elaborated code'. (p.93)

Trudgill goes on to caution strongly against confusing non-standard dialect with 'restricted code'. This confusion is one means by which non-standard dialects are devalued.

These last two sections will have raised several questions in the minds of teachers. Perhaps the principal one will be that of how to proceed in the case of children with markedly non-standard dialects. An argument is often made that academic success depends on being able to deal with

Standard English, which is the medium of school textbooks and a good deal of teaching. Trudgill, in his book, provides a discussion of the various approaches which have been taken.

To quote from his conclusions:

. . . the only legitimate motive for teaching children to speak standard English as a second dialect is to prevent them being discriminated against for speaking socially stigmatised dialects; and the only legitimate method of teaching it is to use the bi-dialectalism approach. (p.79)

In the case of writing, Trudgill allows that there are legitimate arguments that children should be able to produce Standard English, in that it is used almost universally in formal writing. Trudgill, however, doubts the value of teaching spoken standard English in schools:

The teaching of spoken standard English in school is not advisable, since it is almost certainly a waste of time. (p.79)

We suggest that there is room for a compromise position here and that it may be possible and valuable to teach the child who has a particularly strong localised dialect a set of alternative ways of 'saying the same thing'. This is probably the commonsense position that most teachers have always taken. It is certainly noticeable, in many parts of the country, that teachers themselves speak a form of English which has lots of local features but which is nearer to Standard English than the forms used by their pupils. The teacher is often quite unaware that these local features are not ordinary Standard English. The model which the teacher offers in spoken English is, then, quite likely not to be strictly Standard English but it is clearly adequate for communicating comfortably with people who come from outside the immediate dialect area. It is obviously essential not to give the pupil the impression that his dialect is in any way inferior or that the child should 'not speak like that'. It is, however, equally essential for any child who is to have any hope of progress in the educational system, and of eventually being a fit applicant for a job which involves talking to people who come from outside the immediate dialect area, to be able to control a form of spoken English which is comprehensible to 'outsiders'. Children in our educational system ought to have the right to such a hope. They ought at least to understand that 'outsiders' may have difficulty in understanding some local forms and that in talking to such outsiders more generally understood forms are appropriate.

It is not our remit in this book to suggest how such a programme of flexible language usage should be implemented. We merely note that most adolescents are quite familiar with and quite able to produce more widely understood forms. What seems to be at issue is not so much 'knowing the forms' as recognising the appropriate occasions for their use and being prepared to use them.

2.3 'Having language'

In the last section we discussed the view which many people have drawn from Bernstein's original 'restricted/elaborated code' distinction, which is that some children, particularly working class children, have in some sense 'less language' available to them than other, particularly middle class, children. Since our own work leads us to believe that there is no reason to suppose that there is any significant difference in the *amount* of language which different speakers 'have', we shall briefly consider what it means to 'have' language.

If 'having language' is taken to mean knowing a set of words of the language (vocabulary), knowing a set of the possible syntactic structures of the language (grammar), knowing how to pronounce sentences composed of words (pronunciation) and knowing how to use the language appropriately to perform culturally recognised acts (apologising, thanking, warning, advising, conversing, requesting, etc.), then we have no reason to believe that an educationally unsuccessful 16 year-old has any less language than an academically successful 16 year-old. Both pupils will know an immense amount of vocabulary – though it may be that the academically successful pupil may know, or may use, more vocabulary which is highly valued within an educational setting. Both pupils will know, and be capable of manipulating, most of the syntactic structures of English which characterise their particular dialect, though the academically successful pupil may use in speaking more of the forms which are more typical of the written language. Both pupils will be able to pronounce what they want to say. Both pupils will be able to perform a similar range of culturally recognised tasks (though one may be perceived within the school setting as being more socially competent than the other – a perception which may have little to do with the pupil's use of language or relative educational success). If we were to think, in simple-minded terms, of each pupil having a language bucket, we have no reason to suppose that one pupil has more in his language bucket than the other.

A number of educational experiments have been carried out in the past which have assumed that because a pupil did not produce a particular form, or type of form, in the experimental context, the pupil did not 'have' that form. It is important to realise that, if a pupil does not produce say, a passive construction, in a particular task, the most we can say is that the particular speaking situation was not one which elicited passives from that pupil: it does not allow us to infer that the pupil cannot produce passives under other circumstances. We may appeal here to the notion introduced into linguistics by Noam Chomsky: the distinction between 'competence', the knowledge of his language which an individual has in his head, and 'performance', the language displayed by an individual on an occasion of use.

The point which we shall reiterate throughout this book is that it does not seem necessary to teach native speakers their own language. They know their own language. What is necessary is to teach them appropriate occasions of use for the language forms that they already know, to deploy their language effectively.

2.4 Theories of verbal deprivation and deficit

2.4.1 Sensory deprivation

The incorporation of the idea of 'sensory deprivation' into theories of remedial education, in the 1960s, was a clear case of incorrectly drafting a psychological term into another discipline; the danger mentioned at the beginning of this chapter.

The term 'sensory deprivation' was in use in psychology at the time to describe the conditions of lack of light, sound and tactile stimulation used in certain experiments. The experiments typically consisted of rearing newborn animals in these conditions in order to assess the influence of the environment on perceptual, cognitive and social development; there were also the well known experiments in which people were deprived of practically all sensory stimulation for a few hours in order to investigate the temporary disturbances in their cognitive functioning. For some people – mostly in America – this notion was an attractive one to apply to child development, particularly in the light of research which had compared very young children in institutions such as state-run orphanages providing only minimal physical care with those living at home. This research revealed that the children in the latter were developing faster – sitting up, standing, walking, talking – than the children in the institutions; an explanation was seen in the fact that these children received more attention, had more toys and were generally in a richer environment.

So, the term 'sensory deprivation' was drafted in to explain the educational disadvantage suffered by many working class children at school. This 'fad' – as Bereiter and Engelmann called it – had it that working class children suffer because, in the first couple of years of life, they are exposed to less sensory stimulation than middle class children. Hence, they do not develop as quickly or as far. The following criticism, taken from Bereiter and Engelmann (1966), shows why this particular theory had only a limited life.

It would seem that those who have attributed sensory deprivation to lower class children have not seriously considered what the term implies. It has nothing to do with the educational quality of the stimuli available, but only with their variety, intensity and patterning. On these purely quantitative bases, automobiles passing in the street are as good as story books, old shoes are as good as dolls, and trash cans are as good as toy drums.   (Bereiter and Englemann, *Teaching disadvantaged children in the pre-school*, p.27)

The idea of 'deprivation' has been applied to child development, and language learning in particular, in other, rather more sophisticated ways, which we will now consider.

2.4.2 Cultural deprivation

A more resilient notion has been that of 'cultural deprivation'. According to this theory, some children may be labelled as disadvantaged because, in their very early years, they were 'deprived' of many of the elements of the middle class culture on which most educational practice is based. The research on cultural deprivation is rather vague on what it is that the child's early socialisation lacks. In the main, the child is seen as not having the appropriate attitudes to learning and to work, or the appropriate motivation and aspirations. 'Culturally deprived' children are also seen as having had insufficient exposure to various types of communication, and hence to be lacking in many communication skills. Deprivation affecting the child's language will be looked at more thoroughly in the next section.

In short, the child is said to be deficient in certain rather high-level skills and dispositions because of lack of exposure to them in the very early years. Most of the research framed in terms of this theory is descriptive rather than explanatory, though. No great impression has been made on the very complex ways in which the elements of the early social environment – the attitudes and influences of parents, siblings and peers – interact to shape the child that enters school. Most of these studies directly or indirectly point to working class culture and living conditions as being responsible for creating educational disadvantage; in some respects it is legitimate to make such judgments from the perspective of middle class values (in that these are the values of the school in many cases), but often the research seems to contain no conscious recognition of this.

It follows from the theory that we have certain children who are *deficient* in certain respects as a result of an early environment which *deprived* them of certain influences. Note that this locates the faults within the child and the child's own culture, and the faults are that certain things are lacking. This way of thinking about educational disadvantage formed the backdrop for all of the American programmes of intervention and compensatory education; perhaps the best known of these was the Head Start programme in the late 1960s.

The main opposition to this way of thinking has come from researchers who have pointed out that cultures are different to each other, not inferior or superior. Accepting this relativistic theory means that the terrain of the argument shifts away from talking about *deficits* in children, and moves towards the idea of *differences* between children. It means that the child's native dialect is not under-valued and, if it is judged desirable to encourage the child to adopt a more standard dialect in certain situations (for written work, for instance, or for formal speech – as in an interview), then this is presented as the adoption of an additional way of speaking or writing, rather than as a use of language which in all contexts is superior to the child's native dialect.

2.4.3 Verbal deprivation

The previous two sections on theories of deprivation which have interested educationalists have really been leading up to this section on 'verbal deprivation' – something which is directly relevant to the interests of this book. A common view from the mid-1960s onwards was that children who were at an educational disadvantage were often, crucially, deficient in their use of language. As with the broader theory of cultural deprivation, they were seen as having a deficit as a result of their deprived backgrounds. In this case, though, the deficit was a verbal one: what they were assumed to be deprived of was the middle class speech environment which prepared middle class children so well for the type of language which they would encounter at school

Most of this theorising was done by researchers and educationalists who were anxious to provide lower class pre-school children with some kind of 'compensatory education' so that they would be able to begin school on more equal terms. (Note that there was no question of deprivation of written language; the deprivation – and the deficit – were thought to be of spoken language.) Although a number of language remediation projects have been undertaken in Britain, many of the more influential ones were conducted in America. The researchers and teachers who were

involved in this work were not only different from their subjects by virtue of a middle class/lower class divide, but there was also often a black/
white divide, as many of the lower class children selected for such projects were black. Thus, Bereiter and Engelmann, in 1966 in a report of
the progress of their pre-school language remediation project, interpret
the speech of black children as being deficient to the entent that such
children do not appear to have language, or be able and willing to use it to
describe and express things, in the same way that non-black, non-lower
class children do. Bereiter and Engelmann say:

The speech of the severely deprived children seems to consist not of distinct
words, as does the speech of middle class children of the same age, but rather of
whole phrases or sentences that function like giant words. That is to say, these
'giant word' units cannot be taken apart by the child and re-combined; they cannot be transformed from statements to questions, from imperatives to declara-
tives, and so on. Instead of saying 'He's a big dog', the deprived child says 'He
bih daw'. Instead of saying 'I ain't got no juice', he says 'Uai-ga-na-ju'. Instead of
saying 'That is a red truck', he says 'Da-re-truh'.

They continue:

Once the listener has become accustomed to this style of speech, he may begin to
hear it as if all the sounds were there, and may get the impression that he is hearing articles when in fact there is only a pause where the article should be. He may
believe that the child is using words like *it*, *is*, *if*, and *in*, when in fact he is using
the same sound for all of them – something on the order of 'ih'. (p.34)

One should remember that the children whose speech they are describing are normal children with no hearing or articulatory problems;
'severely deprived' refers to the 'verbal deprivation' in their early environment. As for the 'distinct words' spoken by middle class children, it is
an interesting exercise to take a tape of normal, adult or child conversational speech, and try to excise what should be the individual words. The
excised portions can then be spliced back into a blank tape and listened
to. Without the surrounding sentence to aid in their identification, it is
surprising how indistinct, often unrecognisable, many of the words are:
small, common words (the 'closed class' words like articles and preposi-
tions) are almost always mere hiccoughs when listened to on their own.
That is to say, Bereiter and Engelmann's remarks will apply to all natural
speech, not just to that of lower class speakers.

When speech is listened to, the listener contributes a great deal. It is
not simply a case of passively registering each of the words in the incom-
ing speech and then working out what is being said. Speech perception –
the picking out of the actual words – is a very active process. The speech
is usually accompanied by a lot of extraneous non-speech noise, such as

the sound of traffic, birdsong, chairs scraping, people coughing and so on, and very often there is competing speech when other people are speaking nearby. To add to the difficulty, there is always 'distortion' in normal speech – the words run together, the edges of them become indistinct or vanish altogether, the unstressed syllables of words are reduced to a neutral hum. (As an example of this last fact, note that the spelling of the word 'separate' is often found to be a problem because the second syllable is unstressed and is reduced in normal conversation to a neutral sound which does not remind one of an 'a' or an 'e'.)

A small amount of this 'distortion' is actually realised in the written form, in words such as 'gonna', 'wanna', 'can't' and 'I'll' and in phrases such as 'drinka pinta milka day'.

It is a characteristic of speech perception that it has to do a great deal of 'cleaning up' and 'patching up' of the signal before a string of 'distinct words' is arrived at. We have already said that small, common words such as 'the', 'a', 'to', 'in', 'it' and so on, are almost always unrecognisable when they are excised from a tape of normal speech and listened to on their own; nevertheless, these words appear to be just as real to the listener as any of the other words. This is as a result of the reconstruction that occurs when speech is perceived. Normally this reconstruction is a process which we are unaware of; it is completely automatic. A recognition of this process forms the basis of some of the word-play games, especially popular with children, for example:

Knock Knock
Who's there?
Senior
Senior who?
Senior so nosey, I shan't tell you.

One popular criticism levelled against certain non-standard speech is that it is 'unclear' or 'indistinct'. As we have seen, this criticism is misplaced, in that conversational speech in Standard English is no more 'distinct'. In fact, it is the degree to which the listener is acquainted with the language and the dialect being spoken which will determine how easily the listener can cope with understanding the speech. This fact is recognised in the earlier quotation from Bereiter and Engelmann ('Once the listener has become accustomed to this style of speech, he may begin to hear it as if all the sounds were there . . .'). A dialect speaker will have the same problems when first listening to the standard form of the language, as a speaker of the standard form when first confronted with dialect speech. An infant learning a language as its native tongue does not suffer because the dialect it is exposed to is non-standard; all dialects, including standard ones, present the same task to the infant who is acquiring the language.

Returning, after that short detour through speech perception to the issue of the language remediation components of compensatory education programmes, Edwards (1979) comments that:

> most intervention programmes have suffered from . . . a lack of linguistic awareness . . . (they) are for the most part highly-structured language drills in specific aspects of 'correct' English, and most appear curiously old-fashioned. (p.49, *Language and disadvantage*)

Edwards was referring to intervention programmes such as the Head Start project in the United States, and the Gahagan and Gahagan project in Britain, together with the many smaller ones in both countries. The approach which we take in this book differs crucially from such programmes. Firstly, such remediation programmes have been located more or less explicitly within a 'deficit' view of language differences; this chapter has attempted to show that our approach recognises dialect differences in place of the 'language deficits' of such intervention programmes. Secondly, by strictly defining the scope of our interests as those skills involved in taking long turns in transactional speech, we depart from those intervention programmes which were influenced to varying degrees by Bernstein's early work. Thirdly, as Chapter 1 has made clear, we do not propose 'intervention'. 'Intervention' implies that one is stepping in when a process has gone wrong in some way. What we propose is the *supplementing* of those skills in transactional speech which have already been learned, in the same way that the school continues to supplement and develop *writing* skills once pupils have mastered the basic skills of writing.

Most language remediation programmes have consisted of highly-structured exercises designed to take individual children or groups of children through what are considered to be progressively more advanced stages of language use. Consider the following quotation from Osborn, one of the people involved in implementing the Bereiter and Engelmann programme:

> Backwards practice is helpful for children who leave out small articles and small verbs. The teacher will say 'This is a ball'. Now say this, 'ball', the child says 'ball'; now say, 'a ball', the child says 'a ball' first with the teacher and then by himself. This is repeated several times. The teacher says, 'is a ball', and the child and the teacher repeat this; finally the teacher says 'Let's say the whole thing, This is a ball'.
> (p.42, 'Teaching language to disadvantaged children', in *Language remediation for the disadvantaged pre-school child*, ed. M. Brottman, Monographs of the society for research in child development, 33, No. 8, 1968)

Many of the general criticisms which we have made of such approaches are concretely illustrated in this particular quotation. Firstly, the 'omission' of small articles and small verbs is normal in mature conversational speech; they are not, in fact, being omitted, simply reduced by virtue of being in an unstressed position in the sentence. Because they are highly predictable words in highly predictable positions, the listener is able to 'fill in' the words without noticing. Secondly, the exercise assumes that the child's grasp of language is minimal; it bears repeating that no normal child brought up in a social environment (regardless of the language/dialect spoken) will fail to acquire language.

We might add that this particular exercise appears to have as its aim the remediation of the child's language in abstraction from any particular use; indeed, at one point in the exercise the child is required to produce the interrogative form 'is a ball' when no questioning is taking place. The emphasis is not on speech which is effective in terms of some particular function; instead the emphasis is on speech which conforms to some notion of Standard English as 'correct' English. When children acquire language, they do so as a result of being exposed to a considerable amount of speech from older children and adults. The language which they hear is 'imperfect', in that it is composed mostly of the quite fragmented utterances of everyday conversation, but at least such language is all in the same direction. It is difficult to believe that the 'backwards practice' described by Osborn is motivated by any psychologically realistic theory of language acquisition or language processing. In considering this type of language remediation programme, it seems that we can often add to the charge of linguistic naivety a further charge of psychological naivety.

To draw this section on verbal deprivation to a conclusion: we have looked at the verbal deprivation hypothesis in the context of broader theories of socio-cultural deprivation, and we have seen that it lacks credibility; we have looked at a language remediation programme – a not untypical one at that – based on the notion of verbal deprivation, and seen the type of criticisms which are levelled at such a programme. We shall show in subsequent chapters that it is not the case that all members of the population of 14, 15 and 16 year-olds which we studied were equally skilled in all the verbal tasks which they were given; indeed, many of the performances were far from adequate. The tasks employed were designed to tap definite communication skills and strategies and allow definite conclusions to be drawn from the performances of the pupils. The next section considers what the response should be in the classroom to the situation in which it is judged that not all of the pupils are completely competent with respect to certain communication skills. The skills which contribute to the effective use of spoken language are referred to collectively by the term 'oracy'.

2.5 Developing oracy in the classroom

From the previous sections in this chapter, it is possible to construct a position which says that there should be no intervention at all to change children's language: some children speak differently from other children – that's because of sub-cultural and socio-economic differences – all cultures and sub-cultures are to be valued equally – if anything is to be changed it should be the expectations, practices and prejudices of the school and of society at large. We could call this a 'libertarian' position.

This is not the approach being taken in this book, as will be explained below, but we can consider for a moment what such a libertarian line of argument would have to say about the acquisition of communicative skills. (By 'communicative skills' we mean all those skills above and beyond the 'linguistic competence' involved in creating grammatical sentences; this 'communicative competence' involves all of the social skills necessary for effective and successful conversation and communication.) An argument put forward by Rosen and Rosen, in *The language of primary school children* (1973), suggests the more libertarian approach to acquisition.

This kind of competence (communicative competence) has also to be learned and is no less complex (than linguistic competence) and our point was that some part of this competence can be learned in school not by teaching rules of conversation but by conducting conversation in particular ways. Just as grammatical competence need not be made explicit so communicative competence need not. Similarly, as a child can derive his grammar from what he hears so he can derive his communicative competence from taking part in talk. (p.262)

Previously they say 'We need then to create those situations which exert the greatest pressure on them to use their latent resources, to provide those experiences which urge them towards the widest range of language use' (p.64). Although to a degree it is being suggested that these communicative skills need to be learned in a structured way, in that children (primary school children, in their case) are to be steered towards situations involving different types of communication, there is an explicit assumption that the child will acquire the skills simply by participation, by coming into contact with such skills in others. Admittedly their remarks are qualified by the words 'some part of this competence', but there is in the rest of their remarks the notion that, for example, skill in taking long turns of primarily informative speech is acquired in the same 'automatic' way that skill in taking short turns of primarily social speech is acquired.

Our data show that a considerable proportion of the children who took part in the experiments which we describe could not perform adequately in tasks requiring primarily informative speech; even though they were approaching the end of their school careers (in most of these cases) they had either not had sufficient exposure to the whole range of communicative situations, particularly those involving primarily informative speech, or they had not benefitted from that exposure by developing the relevant skills. As will be seen, our data also indicate that performance in these tasks may be improved in the appropriate circumstances. The only reaction to this can be to say that the school should provide each child with a sufficient amount of speaking experience in situations requiring primarily informative speech, and to follow this exposure with some kind of feedback so that the child understands more about the demands of the task and the specific shortcomings of his own performance, and so that the teacher has some means of assessing the progress of the child and discovering the precise weak spots in the child's developing communicative expertise.

Perhaps we can agree with Rosen and Rosen if we say that some of the expertise that falls under the heading of 'oracy' is acquired apparently effortlessly in the course of interaction with peers and with adults, and that these skills are the skills which contribute towards primarily social speech. All of the children studied in the experiments in this book possessed this kind of expertise in primarily social speech. (Nevertheless, we may speculate that more or less practice with this kind of speech in different situations might produce different levels of expertise.)

The type of teaching of talk which we argue for in this book concerns only the primarily informative speech, which was discussed at length in Chapter 1. Out aim has been to define those skills which contribute to success in different types of informative speech, sometimes with short turns and sometimes with longer turns, and to assess how much they may be developed by practice and by feedback. As with the development of skills in the written language, many children may have the type of home environment which encourages this type of expertise. Nevertheless, if it is clear that teaching can improve the abilities of pupils in terms of those skills which contribute to oracy, then it is the responsibility of the schools to do so.

3 Communicative stress and grading

3.1 The teaching approach

The approach we have adopted in this book is to think of the various skills which we want to inculcate in terms of tasks having different characteristics. In Chapter 4 we discuss the different characteristics of such tasks and how they can be graded. In this chapter we shall, fairly briefly, consider some of the conditions which may have an effect on the language which a pupil is able to produce. These are conditions which, to some extent, it is possible for a teacher to control. Controlling them will give the teacher another parameter of grading. We shall think of them then as conditions in which it is easier or more difficult for a pupil to perform well, which we shall call an index of 'communicative stress'.

3.2 The information gap

Perhaps one of the nicest feelings we experience is knowing some information which we know our listener wants to know but doesn't yet know, and being able to tell the listener what he wants to know – particularly when it's good news. So we all look forward to announcing that some waited-for letter has arrived, that the new baby is a girl, that the driving test was a success. It's always rather a letdown when the listener then lets fall that he already knew what we have told him. Similarly, it's a good feeling when some foreign visitor asks for directions to the castle and we're able to tell him how to get there. Again it would be a curious letdown if he then said 'I already know actually – I was just testing you'.

It's quite a socially daunting experience to tell someone something which you suspect they might know already. If you're having a meal with someone you believe to be an eminent biologist who says he never has understood whether zebras were white animals striped with black or black animals striped with white, even though you know the right answer and the empirical work a friend of yours has just done to demonstrate it, you still may have an uneasy feeling that you are walking on very thin ice as you embark on an account of this work, and are vastly relieved to discover that he's actually an Ear, Nose and Throat specialist. If the driving instructor looks at you with a piercing glint in his eye as you climb into the car at the beginning of your third driving lesson and says 'Right, then, explain to me how the clutch works', even if you think you know, you're likely to feel intimidated. It's much easier to explain to someone who you are sure knows nothing about it, and can't contradict you.

The experience of pupils in the classroom, or in the examination room is clearly relevant here. Typically, they are in the position of telling something to the teacher, who already knows what it is they ought to say. Even as adults, this position may give us a feeling of social unease. The pupil has to make sophisticated judgments about the teacher's assumption of ignorance. How much of what he already obviously knows does he actually need to be explicitly told?

It seems reasonable that we should try to put pupils in the position of talking about information which they have and their listener doesn't have. This may mean that the pupil must be put in the position of informing one of his classmates of something that the classmate doesn't already know.

It is not only the case that it is easier for the pupil to perform well if he is talking to someone who does not know what he knows. It is also important that the person he is talking to should need to know what he knows for some clearly defined purpose. The information gap must be functional. We have suggested that it is easier for the pupil if the gap is not simply constituted by the teacher's being unsure how much the pupil knows on a givèn subject. It is much easier for the speaker if he has to tell his listener something which the listener doesn't know but which he needs to know in order to achieve some desired result. One reason why we have chosen to work within a task format is because we can, in each case, specify a task which the listener is asked to complete as a result of the information which he is given by the speaker. We provide the listener and, thus, the speaker, with a motivation for transferring information.

3.3 The listener

When we discussed comfortable chat, in Chapter 1, we pointed out that one reason why much chat is comfortable is because the speaker feels at ease with his listener. It seems clear that pupils generally feel more at ease talking to each other than talking to a teacher or to some other adult, no matter how kind and sympathetic the adult may be. The advantage of talking to another individual who shares the same daily experiences which you have and sees them from a very similar point of view, is that you can take so much background knowledge for granted. You don't have to keep spelling out your assumptions about the nature of the world because they're already established between you. This is presumably why we, as adults, in a gathering of friends, tend to drift towards close colleagues and sooner or later end up 'talking shop'. It is so restful to talk to people whose experience largely overlaps with yours. The converse of this, of course, is living for a while in a foreign community. While it may be constantly interesting, exciting and stimulating, many people also find that it's extremely tiring, precisely because you have to spend so much time explaining or finding out the reason for trivial habits, phrases, ways of looking at things.

In our experience pupils perform best on the tasks which we shall describe in the next chapter, when they are talking to a friend from the same class. They are interactionally at ease and relaxed. They chat to begin with and then pay full attention to the task, occasionally commenting and making witty remarks to each other. They perform better under these circumstances than they do with an adult interviewer, even if they have chatted apparently quite happily to the interviewer before the task began. In the following excerpt Speaker A sounds as if he's enjoying the task of telling B how to draw a route on the 'map' of an island:

(1) A: you go over to quite a bit below the bottom of the swamp
    B: what swamp?
    A: swamp swamp
    B: how far is it away from Palm Beach?
    A: about forty miles (giggles) + it's quite a big bit away

We should also note that pupils perform better when they are talking directly to a friend than they do when they are asked to talk into a microphone so that the message could be played to a friend, who would then perform the task. We experimented with this mode of task presentation because it is one which is apparently used quite a lot in some schools, particularly for assessment purposes. In general pupils produced less talk, and less adequate talk, when they spoke into the microphone. In instructional tasks, for instance, they spoke more quickly, left inadequate pauses, failed to distinguish the components adequately or to express the relationships adequately. It's important to consider this effect, since it means that pupils, asked to perform under these circumstances, are likely to perform much less well than they are capable of performing in more normal conditions of language use when their listener is physically present. (We have not experimented with pupils talking over the telephone which might at first blush seem rather similar to talking into a microphone. One important difference between these conditions must be that the speaker speaking into a microphone receives no feedback from his listener, whereas a speaker talking into a telephone would normally expect to receive feedback – comments like 'yes', 'right', 'OK', 'uhuh', 'mmm', 'hold on', 'you're going too fast', etc.)

The conditions under which speakers are placed when they talk to each other have an effect on their feeling of comfort in an interaction. There is little doubt that people feel most comfortable sitting companionably side by side, or at 90° to each other at the corner of a table. The problem for our procedure is that we don't want the speaker and listener to be able to look over at each other's information, since we are concerned with transferring information verbally. We have sometimes used an experimental arrangement where a pair of pupils sits back to back but this has to be said to look very unnatural, even though pupils perform perfectly well in this condition. With a number of pairs sitting together in a classroom like this, the result would probably be an unholy din. The most satisfactory arrangement appears to be where speaker and listener face each other across a table, so they can talk quietly to each other, nod, smile, and have normal conversational eye-contact, but where there is a low screen (or propped-up open folder) which prevents the listener from seeing the speaker's information and the speaker from pointing to what the listener is doing. This arrangement is clearly not a natural one but one can readily think of many occasions in real life where there is indeed a rather similar physical barrier – talking to bank, post office or booking office officials who are sitting behind a glass screen are obvious examples, describing your symptoms to the doctor on the other side of the table who is jotting them secretively down on his pad, or trying to describe to the sales assistant behind the counter what it is that your television is doing that isn't right. We have used this format satisfactorily both for pupils working co-operatively together, where both may talk, and in assessment procedures where only the nominated speaker does the talking.

One dimension of grading communicative stress would be to begin with pupils talking to one other pupil, to move later to pupils addressing small groups of three or four, and eventually to addressing the class, or unfamiliar adults, and so on. A further listener variable, not one which we have attempted to incorporate yet, is the preparedness of the listener to leave the speaker plenty of time to work out what he wants to say. It is more stressful for the speaker if his listener is in a hurry or is impatient with what he is saying. As adults in the real world we often need to formulate messages in a hurry, or to speak to listeners in a superior role. A lot of work in the past few years has shown the difficulty experienced by patients in communicating with doctors and by witnesses answering questions in court. Even normally competent speakers find such situations stressful. Some speakers in such stressful conditions may simply fail to communicate what they want to say or positively misrepresent what they want to say. It seems at least possible that practice in role-play with an impatient listener might usefully be incorporated in a spoken language syllabus, once the pupil has reached a fair degree of competence in communicating in a relatively non-stressful situation.

We mentioned earlier the possibility of organising discussion in small groups. This is certainly useful experience for pupils. It is, however, an activity which, in the present state of our knowledge of group dynamics, would probably not offer the teacher much opportunity for improving a pupil's performance. It is known that individuals tend to adopt particular roles in small groups – so Mary may adopt the leading authoritative role in a particular group and Jimmy may adopt the role of the witty, anti-establishment, one-liner. In a different group, with a different 'group chemistry', Mary may adopt a supportive listener role or she may take the role which Jimmy played in the first group. Some groups may fail to 'gel' and produce very little talk, while another may contain two individuals vying for the authoritative role who give others very little chance of participating. It is very hard to see how we would judge the value of a particular individual's contribution. Being a sympathetic listener, who says very little, if anything, may be as important to the social cohesiveness of the group as being an active talker. In a 20 minute video film of a group of six children having a discussion with their teacher one pupil made only two remarks in the entire session. Yet in each case the remark initiated a really interesting development of the topic. How would we assess such a contribution against that made by another child who chattered on, in a not particularly interesting way, but succeeded in maintaining a cheerful talking atmosphere in the group?

In group discussion it may only be possible for the teacher to observe, in an impressionistic way, that one pupil often talks a lot and talks sensibly and that another listens carefully and that another keeps making irrelevant remarks.

3.4 Task type

We shall discuss details of many different task types in Chapter 4. All we want to do here is to point out that many of the tasks which we describe, just like many familiar classroom tasks, are actually cognitively very difficult. One difficulty often lies in the problem that the speaker has in assessing the amount of background knowledge which he may assume his listener shares with him. (Note that we are not speaking here of the 'information gap' with respect to the specific information to be transferred but of how much the speaker can assume the listener knows in general about this type of event.) A second difficulty often lies in the problem of constructing a reportable event out of what is felt to be a relatively unstructured experience. We shall discuss each of these difficulties in turn.

3.4.1 Sharing background knowledge

When you meet someone on the train and they ask you what you do for a living, depending on what it is you do, there is often a sinking of the heart. If you do some sort of job which most members of the community know about – schoolteacher, doctor, lawyer, bus conductor, hairdresser – you may think there's no problem at all. If, however, you do something out of the ordinary like work for the British Council, or manufacture nymphs or teach linguistics you have a problem on your hands. If you confess what you do, the inevitable next question asks you what that involves. At this point you have to make a sophisticated judgment about what the person you are talking to is likely to know about that relates to what you do, which will enable him to get some not-too-distorted view of the sort of thing you do. If you're feeling strong you may take this as an interesting imaginative feat, but if you're not, you probably try to give a minimal answer and turn the conversation towards an area where you both share background knowledge.

Consider now the problem when you ask a pupil to tell the class about something he knows about. Some pupils can cope with this, but many find such an experience intimidating. One of the problems of addressing a large group is that background knowledge is unevenly distributed among its constituent members. Suppose the pupil is asked to describe how he spends an evening at karate class. It may be that no one else actually goes to karate class, so in that sense the pupil may feel relatively confident of the information gap. However, he may know that several of his friends, but not all of them, have seen a film on television about karate. It's quite difficult for him to judge how much background detail he's to give which won't, on the one hand, bore those who have seen the film or, on the other, mystify those who haven't seen the film. Certainly, advanced pupils might be required to undertake such a task. For novices in long turn management, it is very demanding to try to imagine and to keep in mind different amounts of knowledge among your audience.

Many apparently straightforward tasks which require the speaker to talk about something which he knows about, and his listeners don't, make this complex demand on the speaker. Thus a speaker asked to give an account of an evening at Scouts, a film on television, an outing to a coalmine, a holiday in Blackpool, how to play table tennis, will, in each case, have to consider how much background knowledge his listener is likely to have – the situation is, we have suggested, even more complex if there are several listeners. In some situations, particularly one-to-one interaction among peers, the speaker may feel confident enough to try to find out how much, if anything, his listener shares as background knowledge by asking him whether, for example, he's ever been to Blackpool or, if not, has he ever been to some other English seaside town. If the topic is something the speaker knows about very well and he is not sympathetic to the possible lack of knowledge on the part of his listener, he is likely to impute far too much knowledge to his listener – as did the speaker in extract (7) in Chapter 1, who talked about *Jaws*. Learning to take account of the listener's state of knowledge is obviously a listener-related skill but one which is essential to satisfactory transfer of information. Most pupils will require training in this skill.

3.4.2 Chunking experience

Many of the apparently simple tasks we mentioned in the last section require the speaker to review some experience like 'an evening at Guides' or 'a holiday in Blackpool' and abstract from that total experience some portion which can be detached and presented meaningfully on its own. Suppose a pupil has been on holiday to France. Many teachers might take the opportunity of asking the pupil to tell the class about this holiday. Such a task actually demands extremely skillful judgment on the part of the speaker. It's very hard to abstract a piece of experience and 'make a story' of it.

This phenomenon is very familiar to the parents of small children. Many parents beam at the child as he returns from his first day at primary school, and say 'What did you do today?'. There is, typically, a long pause, and then the child screws out some statement about a banal activity like 'we had dinner' or 'I went to the toilet'. It seems that the child has classified such events as whole events which can be talked about. They have a structure which relates to the child's previous experience of life. But at this point the child has no names for the new unstructured experiences of the day and is virtually incapable of talking about them. That same problem remains when someone asks you what you did on holiday – the answers are usually a banal list of familiar events, which the speaker knows the listener will be able to recognise from the names he uses for them. Suppose the pupil, standing in front of the class, tries to talk about his holiday in France. He has to organise his experience into chunks which can be identified and talked about. If he is talking to someone who shared the experience, there is no problem – there are signposts in memory which can be mentioned and which will revive an entire shared event, but to communicate successfully with someone who hasn't shared the experience is a sophisticated and demanding task. The problems lie both in abstracting 'tellable' chunks of experience and in determining how much background knowledge the listeners are likely to have about the events being talked about.

3.4.3 Grading task types

In Chapter 4 we shall discuss some of the formal properties of different types of task. At this point we simply reiterate that many of the essay type topics which pupils are asked to talk about are particularly difficult for the inexperienced speaker to control. The selection of necessary information (in terms of what the listener may be expected to know), and of 'reportable' information, and structuring that into an interesting account is an acquired skill. We suggest that, at the beginning of a course, students should not be required to undertake such a complex task in any formal way, certainly not for assessment purposes. Rather they should be trained on relatively simple tasks which offer a lot of support, where the teacher, knowing what it is they need to express, can judge whether or not they have succeeded in doing so and, if not, help them to succeed. Rich, unstructured tasks of the essay type are exceedingly difficult to assess, when presented in the spoken mode to a listener, and it is very hard to see how a teacher could, in any systematic way, start helping a pupil to improve his performance.

3.5 Conditions of input

We have assumed in general that where one pupil has information which he has to impart to a listener, for a purpose, he should not have come by that information in the spoken mode, or certainly not in the spoken mode alone. Early in our investigations we did attempt to provide speakers with information via standard taped input, information which they were then required to pass on to a listener. It quickly became evident that some pupils had much better memories for what they had heard than others. Pupils who were not able to recall what it was they had heard were being penalised in assessment for failure to transfer information which they couldn't remember. It seemed to us important not to confuse the ability to remember (or, perhaps, to understand) what you have heard, with the ability to pass on information using the spoken language, so we abandoned this form of input.

Since that time we have worked largely with visual input to specific tasks, sometimes accompanied by 'pointing' type remarks like 'see this – well it has to fit into this – like that', using in demonstration the sort of language which the pupils themselves control very well, rather than the more explicit language which is necessary when the listener can't see what it is the speaker is doing. Where the listener is assembling, say, an instrument, the speaker has a series of photographs in front of him, showing the assemblage of the instrument, to remind him of the order of assembly, while he is speaking. Where the speaker is relating a narrative, or giving an eye witness account of a theft or an accident, he has a series of drawings or photographs in front of him. Where the speaker is giving instructions about the construction of a wiring diagram, he has an identical diagram in front of him. In each case, our intention is that the memory load is reduced to a minimum. Certainly with this type of presentation we have not had any speakers who have simply given up, which did happen with several pupils who received only an auditory input.

An obviously attractive form of input to a task is to show the pupil a short video film of some event. This has the advantage of being a particularly vivid form of input and it is obvious that pupils in general like working with video. It is important to notice that the vividness of input has to be balanced against the increase in memory load. We have found, particularly with less academically successful pupils, that somewhat less detail is remembered. This suggests that video may be a particularly good input for exercises which require a summary or gist to be produced, but is rather poor input where a detailed account is what is required.

A further variable which may have an effect on the performance of the pupil is the amount of detail in the visual stimulus. The selection of relevant detail from a photograph or cartoon, again constitutes a fairly sophisticated choice. Under what conditions if you see a photograph of the interior of a room do you mention the vase of flowers on top of the television? Under what conditions do you mention that the door of the room is not quite shut? If the instruction is 'tell the listener the name of everything you can see so that he can tick them off in his photograph', it might be appropriate to mention the vase of flowers. If the instruction is 'tell the listener the story you have here so that he can construct a summary of the story for a newpaper article', the vase of flowers shouldn't be mentioned unless it is somehow relevant to the story – for instance if the wife throws it at the husband. The selection of relevant detail is a skill which may need explicit training. One way of grading input would be to use rather bare and simple input at the beginning of the course, and only gradually to move to rich input which demands sophisticated selection by the pupil.

3.6 General advantages of the task-based approach

In Chapter 4 we shall describe a range of tasks and show how different tasks pose different sorts of problems for speakers and give extensive illustration of how speakers succeed or fail in overcoming these problems. At this stage we simply want to point out some of the advantages of adopting a task-based approach. In doing this we shall contrast our approach with other, more traditional and less structured approaches to teaching the spoken language. Naturally we do not wish to suggest that our particular way of doing things is the only appropriate method for teaching spoken language use. Nonetheless it does have several obvious advantages which suggest that it ought to be included as one of the approaches which are available to a teacher.

3.6.1 Benefits of a known input

One familiar method of eliciting talk from a pupil which we discussed in Section 3.4 is to ask him to give a short talk on a particular topic – for instance 'my favourite hobby'. In the tasks we use there is a controlled input and the speaker is asked to draw on that input to give information to a hearer who needs the information for a particular purpose. Simple examples of such tasks would be (i) where the speaker has a diagram in front of him and he has to instruct the hearer how to replicate the diagram and (ii) where the speaker has a series of photographs showing a traffic accident in front of him and has to report the accident to the hearer so that the hearer can fill out an insurance claim. In such tasks, the content to be communicated is known to the teacher. The teacher knows that, in the diagram task, a certain number of items have to be described, and that a speaker cannot perform the task successfully without informing the hearer about all of them. The teacher's knowledge of the content to be communicated makes it possible to set criteria for a successful performance. How does the teacher judge what a pupil ought to say in a talk about football? Does the pupil have to mention that the game is played with a ball? If the speaker omits this is he making the reasonable assumption that the audience already knows that football involves a ball or is this a failure on the speaker's part? Such a lack of clearly defined content presents the teacher with problems in assessing whether such a talk is successful in terms of communicating an adequate amount of information.

The known content and structure of the input materials also mean that the outputs produced by speakers are directly comparable. Each speaker is facing a task of equal difficulty since each speaker has the same information to communicate to the hearer. In free talks, it may well be the case that one speaker has a real advantage because, for example, it may be easier to describe disco dancing, than it is to explain the enjoyment of scuba diving. The teacher then has problems in assessing whether it is the relative ease or difficulty of the unknown content or the skills of the speakers which result in good or poor performances.

The task-based approach has several real advantages from the viewpoint of diagnostic assessment. As the input can be analysed before any pupil performs the task, an objective assessment procedure can be devised which lists the information which the speaker must mention to complete the task successfully. This list forms a scoring protocol which can then be applied to all performances equally and a quantifiable evaluation can be made of how well each speaker communicated the required information. (In Chapter 5 we will describe in more detail the assessment procedures we have devised for a range of tasks.)

Performances on structured tasks can, of course, be used to assess other aspects of talk besides information transferring ability. A teacher can use the same performance to evaluate impressionistically any number of features of his own interest; fluency, grammatical correctness, range of vocabulary, etc. and, again, the comparable nature of the task and the length of talk elicited may also be advantageous for these purposes.

3.6.2 Advantages of the task-based approach in teaching

Teaching pupils to communicate effectively is a matter of general concern. Teaching implies the ability to diagnose particular problems. We believe that the task-based approach offers real benefits in this respect. Our main interest in developing the assessment procedures described in Chapter 5, is that a good reliable method of assessment allows teachers to identify areas where pupils are having problems and then to direct teaching effort towards remediating these problems.

How might such diagnostic assessment and remediation work in practice? If a teacher is trying to encourage pupils to give clear and precise instructions, he might present a pupil with a simple diagram and ask him to instruct a hearer how to draw it. If this performance is then assessed with the aid of a scoring protocol, the teacher can determine if the speaker has successfully mentioned all the required information, or if the speaker has not been completely successful, he can identify exactly what kind of information is being omitted. Ideally, the teacher would play the taped performance to the speaker and the hearer, with the two diagrams in view, and discuss how the instructions given, or those not given, have resulted in similar or different diagrams. In Chapter 6 we describe a study we conducted which shows that pupils can make significant improvements following such discussions and experience in both the speaker's and hearer's role in such a task. The scoring protocol provides a handy outline to focus the pupil's attention on what kind of information the speaker needs to provide in the instructions if the task is to be completed successfully.

The task-based approach allows the teacher to offer the speaker a subsequent opportunity to attempt a similar sort of task but one which is different in its detailed content, so that the pupil can put the lessons learned from a first performance into practice. This is probably more acceptable to most pupils than the repetition involved in rehearsing or preparing a talk where the content is basically the same on each performance.

Using the 'free talk' method, the alternative to repetition is to ask the speaker to produce a second, different, talk. While this overcomes the problems of boredom involved in straight repetition, any lessons learned about the adequacy or inadequacy of a first performance may be quite hard for the speaker to generalise to a talk on a completely different topic.

3.6.3 Tasks of graded levels of difficulty

In the task-based approach, we are concerned with offering pupils opportunities to demonstrate and to improve their communication skills. To this end we have devised alternative versions of tasks which can be used by the teacher in the way just described. We have devised tasks which not only have alternative versions, but which also have versions at different levels of difficulty. This means that the teacher who is interested in developing the communication skills associated with a particular type of task, can present a pupil with a version of that task, of a known level of difficulty. If the pupil is assessed as performing this task fairly well, with perhaps only minor omissions of relevant information, after discussion of the performance, the pupil can be offered an alternative version of the task at the same level of difficulty. If this second performance is more successful the teacher can later present the pupil with more difficult versions of the same task type. Again in Chapter 6 we describe the benefits which the speaker derives from having experience of tasks in ascending order of difficulty. As we shall show in more detail in Chapter 5, a pupil's course record will note the level of difficulty successfully achieved on each type of task.

However, if an initial performance on a particular task type is fairly unsuccessful, and after discussion the second performance on an alternative task shows that the pupil still has real problems with this level of difficulty, the teacher can select an easier version of the same type of task for the pupil to attempt. The two performances can then be compared, and the speaker's more successful performance at the easier level can be used to demonstrate how the more difficult level should be tackled. For example, if a speaker in telling a story which involves four female characters, uses the same expression 'the woman' or 'she' to refer to each of the different characters, the hearer will probably not be able to understand the story. The performance shows that the speaker has a specific problem in discriminating between a number of same-gender characters. The speaker could then be given a story which is considerably easier in terms of the characters involved. For example, he might be given the story (described in Section 4.1.3 in the next chapter) where there are only two female characters, who look very different in the stimulus pictures. In telling this story most speakers are likely to choose different expressions to refer to the two female characters. As this story involves fewer characters, the speaker is also more likely than in the more difficult story to be consistent in the way he identifies the characters throughout the story. However, if the performance on this story is also unsuccessful, the stimulus pictures contain only a few potential trouble spots to be discussed with the speaker while listening to his performance. Stimulus materials for an alternative easy story could then be examined and potentially confusing pictures highlighted before this task is tackled, thus maximising the speaker's chances of success. We have found that the confidence and insights gained from a successful performance on an easy level task allow the speaker to go on to achieve success at more difficult levels.

In Chapter 6, we discuss examples which show how certain easily manageable conditions can result in improved communicative performances even without the benefits of explicit teaching. Such conditions, combined with the kind of classroom practice just described, will allow the teacher to elicit from even the least confident pupils, performances which demonstrate real progress in the development of communicative skills. By using tasks of graded levels of difficulty, the teacher maximises the pupil's chances of making progress. If the 'free talk' method is used, it is much less obvious how such progress could be demonstrated. Although some topics for talks seem more difficult than others, for example, 'using a home computer', versus 'playing football', or 'why I enjoyed Romeo and Juliet' versus 'what I did on holiday', it is hard for the teacher to define what it is that is difficult, in a way which will help the speaker who is not producing 'good' talks on these difficult topics. It is even harder to see in what way the easier talks could be used to demonstrate how the pupil should tackle the more difficult ones.

How is the pupil, particularly the less able or less confident pupil, to grasp what constitute the criteria for a good performance on such talks? If the pupil is not being 'interesting' or 'fluent', what can the teacher point to in the performance which the pupil can remedy? If the pupil in a graded instructional task is not being sufficiently informative, the teacher can point to the differences in the diagram drawn by the hearer, or to the piece of equipment incorrectly assembled, to illustrate how omitting certain information caused problems. The teacher can illustrate the difference between a successful and an unsuccessful performance in a specific way. The objective criteria for success can be applied equally to all the performances in the class, and pupils can compare the particular points of difference which led to more or less successful performances.

If a pupil hears several 'free talks' from his classmates on different topics and he hears the teacher's evaluative comments on these, he might still be unclear as to what were the crucial distinctions among the talks. Did speaker A do well because bird-watching was a 'better' hobby than disco dancing? Did speaker B gain marks because he talked for over five minutes ? Was speaker C penalised for being boring about fishing, when fishing must be a pretty boring hobby anyway? Did speaker D concentrate so much on 'not mumbling' that he sounded really bored with what he was saying ? How does the teacher weight the criteria of fluency/interest/information?

We do not suggest that it is impossible to conceive of a system of analysis which would enable us to grade levels of difficulty in 'free talks' and to develop diagnostic criteria which would permit the teacher to identify a pupil's specific difficulties, so that they could be remedied. So far, no such system is available. At the moment, the best that the teacher can do is to apply the sorts of criteria which have been applied to essay-marking to the delivery of such 'free talks'. This is not a reason for abandoning them as an exercise, though it does seem likely that, for reasons which we have gone into in this chapter, less confident, less 'articulate', pupils may find them particularly difficult, and may not learn very much from the experience.

A more systematic approach to training communicative skills, which permits a pupil to progress from less demanding to more demanding tasks, and which permits the teacher to identify problems and train the pupil to overcome them seems, at the very least, a necessary corrective addition to any curriculum which proposes to take teaching spoken English seriously.

4 Types of task

4.1 The task-based approach to eliciting information-related talk

In this chapter, we describe in some detail the methods which we have used to elicit a variety of types of informative talk from a large number of teenage speakers. We believe that the task-based approach, although apparently rather different from usual practices in English teaching, has great advantages in the teaching and assessing of this aspect of talk. These advantages are discussed at some length in Sections 3.6 to 3.6.3. At this stage, we shall describe our own initial reasons for adopting this approach, because we believe that the problems a teacher faces in devising a new syllabus in a new area of English teaching, may be similar to the problems which we as researchers in this field have had to overcome.

The first problem which we were concerned with was motivating the pupils to talk, with an unfamiliar interviewer and whilst being tape-recorded. We were particularly concerned with whether we would be able to elicit performances from the less academically able teenagers who might not in general be highly motivated to perform or more crucially, to perform to the best of their abilities, under these circumstances. We decided that a series of short tasks, conducted under the ideal conditions described in Chapter 3, with different content and different demands would be more likely to sustain the interest and attention of most pupils. We have found that this variety has paid dividends. In hundreds of hours of recordings, nearly all speakers produce extended talk which is relevant to the task and which, both in content and style of delivery, suggests an earnest attempt by the speaker to complete the task successfully. There are, of course, many performances which we might assess as less than fully successful, but we are fairly confident that few of these result from lack of motivation on the speaker's part.

Our second problem, derived in part from the solution we adopted to our first, namely the variety of the tasks presented. We wanted a wide selection of tasks both to motivate our speakers and to sample from a wide range of information-transferring situations, but we did not wish to end up with a hotchpotch of unrelated performances from which no general description could be drawn of a pupil's, or a group of pupils', abilities. So we devised tasks which formed related groups, each depending on a particular communicative skill. Many tasks which are very different in format and content, and so are useful in retaining the pupil's interest, provided us with information about a pupil's ability on a restricted range of information-transferring skills. In Sections 4.1.2 to 4.1.4, the particular demands of different types of task are discussed in detail.

In Appendix A, we list many of the tasks we have used successfully to elicit particular kinds of informative speech. At present let us consider three of these tasks: a diagram-drawing task, a pegboard task, and a wiring-board task. These three tasks are apparently very different. In the diagram-drawing task, the speaker has to instruct his hearer how to draw a particular coloured diagram. In the pegboard task, the speaker has to tell the hearer how to arrange coloured pegs and coloured elastic bands on a pegboard in a particular pattern and in the wiring-board task, the speaker has to instruct the hearer how to arrange a series of wires in the appropriate sockets to complete an electric circuit.

These tasks differ in the content to be communicated and in their 'real worldliness' but are in fact similar in the communicative demands they pose. To perform these tasks successfully, the speakers must demonstrate the basic information-transferring skills of being clear and explicit in their instructions. The speaker has to tell the hearer exactly what to do. If a line has to be drawn 'under' some feature, or a peg placed 'below' another, or a wire joined to 'a socket', then the speaker has to inform the hearer explicitly how far 'under' or 'below', which wire and which socket is involved, etc. The speaker has to identify and discriminate between sets of objects and express the spatial relationships between them. The same abilities would be involved in many other tasks both in school and in the world at large, such as in describing how a chemistry experiment has to be arranged, explaining how to draw a route on a map, describing how to lay a table correctly, instructing how the stage has to be set in a play, explaining how the dials and meters in an aircraft have to be read, etc.

In all these tasks the speaker cannot assume that the hearer already knows or will be able to guess this information, and if the speaker does make these unwarranted assumptions, we can objectively judge the performance as unsuccessful. In our experimental tasks this can be demonstrated because the hearer will not be able to draw the diagram accurately, arrange the pegboard appropriately, or wire the board correctly. The three apparently different tasks, which we would group together, thus elicit comparable skills from speakers.

4.1.1 Tasks in teaching talk

We have found that different *types* of tasks elicit different types of language and pose different communicative problems for the speaker. From our studies of pupils' performances we have found that there is an ascending scale of difficulty among different task types. Tasks which involve the speaker in describing static relationships among objects are fairly easy to communicate to a hearer, if there are relatively few objects and the relationships between them are fairly simple. Tasks which involve dynamic relationships among people or objects, where a speaker has to describe events which change over time and space, are more difficult. Tasks which require the speaker to communicate abstract notions, for instance in argument or justifications, are more difficult again, for most young speakers.

In Appendix A we describe a range of different spoken language tasks which we have used and the kind of communicative problems they pose. Specific tasks which only require the speaker to describe static relationships include such tasks as:

(i)   Where the speaker has one object or photograph and the hearer has a set of similar objects or photographs. The speaker has to describe the particular object which he has in front of him, so that the hearer can select the matching object from the array of alternatives which he can see.

(ii) Where a speaker is instructing a hearer how to draw a particular diagram so that the hearer's drawing will be identical to the diagram the speaker has in front of him.

(iii) Where a speaker is instructing a hearer how to assemble a piece of equipment.

(iv) Where a speaker is instructing a hearer how to arrange a set of objects.

(v)   Where a speaker is instructing a hearer how to follow route directions.

In these tasks the relationships between the objects are stable. If we take task (ii) as an example, we can see the communicative demands such static tasks require of the speaker. In this task a speaker is given a folder containing a simple diagram (Figure 1a, Appendix A shows one such diagram which we have used extensively). The hearer, who sits opposite, behind a low screen, is given a blank sheet of paper and coloured pens. The speaker is instructed that he has to tell the hearer how to draw the diagram, so that at the end the two diagrams will look *exactly* the same. The speaker is shown the hearer's blank paper and pens to emphasise that the hearer will only have the speaker's instructions for information.

The speaker has to tell the hearer exactly what objects to draw and where on the page these belong. To complete the task successfully, the speaker has to tell the hearer what size, shape and colour each object is and where each has to go in relation to the objects already drawn. In example (1) we see a speaker coping successfully with these requirements. All of these features are stable – the big black square remains a big black square throughout the task. It also remains about an inch under the short red line throughout the task.

In fact in this task the speaker does not even have to give instructions in a particular order. The square can be described first, third or last – it doesn't matter as long as the relevant set of information is included somewhere in the instructions so that the hearer is able to draw a diagram, similar to the one the speaker is describing. In example (2) we see that not all speakers find such tasks easy, even although in this task the information does not have to be ordered in any complex way.

(1) with the black pen nearest the right-hand side of the bit of paper + draw quite a big number three + then about a centimetre and a half down from it with the red pen + draw a + line just about the width of the three + then about two centimetres under that + draw in black pen quite a sort of medium-sized box + then with the red pen about a centimetre down + from underneath the box draw a line + about the width of it

In this performance the speaker is attempting to provide the kind of explicit instructions which the hearer requires to draw the diagram. We would judge that this speaker is performing this task quite successfully, although as we shall see, when we discuss assessing such performances in Chapter 5, the speaker is not quite consistent enough to score full marks. The speaker in (2) in contrast, although starting in a similar way is performing this task rather less well:

(2) on the right-hand side of the paper do a big three + in black pen + and do a red line underneath it + and underneath that + draw a square in black pen + and do a red line underneath that

This speaker does not provide enough information to allow the hearer to draw the diagram accurately. Too many of the later instructions are not specific enough and so we would judge this performance to be less successful than example (1).

In some 'static' tasks, such as assembling a piece of equipment, the information does have to be in a simple linear sequence, but in general in these tasks the main requirement is only that enough information to identify objects and their spatial relationships is provided for the hearer. This information does not have to be described or ordered in any complex way.

4.1.2 Tasks involving dynamic relationships

If we now consider the requirements of tasks involving dynamic relationships, we will see the extra demands which these tasks involve. Tasks such as telling a story, giving an eye witness account of a car crash or recounting how a piece of equipment works, all involve speakers describing relationships which change during the course of the task.

Consider, for example, what is involved in a speaker telling a story, shown in cartoon pictures, to a hearer who cannot see the pictures. Part of one set of such pictures which we have used successfully with many speakers is shown in Figures 3a, b and c, Appendix A (the first three of a set of fourteen pictures are included). In this task, the speaker typically begins by briefly describing the two characters, their relationship, their physical location and activities as shown in Figures 3a – c. When the speaker then describes the later events in the story, in which the man goes to a club or dance, and meets another woman, it must be clear to the hearer, not only what is happening, but also where and when it is happening. The speaker must mention, for example, that the man in the story has gone out/gone to a dance, i.e. that the location has changed. Similarly, the speaker must explain that later events are happening back in the original location shown in pictures a – c, or the hearer may well misunderstand what is happening.

Another interesting aspect of 'dynamic' tasks, is that some of the characters (and/or objects) involved, appear, disappear and reappear, and these changes also have to be clearly and explicitly described by the speaker. For example, in the story we are discussing, the speaker has to make clear to the hearer that the man speaking on the telephone is the same character as the man who was previously at a dance. The speaker must also make it clear that the female character described as listening in the doorway is the *same* female character originally described as sitting reading at the beginning of the story, and that this is a *different* female character from the girl who is now presumably at the other end of the phone. The speaker has to be sufficiently explicit and consistent in the use of language when referring to the various characters in the story to enable the hearer to make this sort of distinction easily.

In a 'static' task, such as the diagram-drawing task, the speaker also has to be referentially explicit, in that if the hearer is told to 'draw a box above the red line', the hearer must be able to decide which red line the speaker is referring to, in order to complete the task successfully. However, in such 'static' tasks, most speakers order their instructions in a simple sequence. The speaker describes one object, for example a red line with its related information (about position on the page, size, etc.) and then uses this feature as a reference point for the next instruction, e.g. 'draw a box above the red line', focussing the hearer's attention on the appropriate line. In these 'static' tasks, the next instruction usually focusses on the next feature, for example, 'above the box draw a short line', so that the hearer's attention is now focussed on the box. If, in a subsequent instruction, the speaker refers to 'the red line' or 'a line', the *sequence* of instructions usually makes it clear which line the speaker is referring to at this point.

In contrast, in the 'dynamic' task, the characters and objects necessarily appear and reappear due to the nature of the stimulus material (for example in the cartoon pictures to be described by the speaker). In these tasks the actual *language* used *must* distinguish which character the speaker is referring to at a particular point in the task.

4.1.3 Examples of performances of speakers in tasks involving dynamic relations

To be successful in a 'dynamic' task the speaker must clearly and consistently describe the characters/objects involved; that is, the speaker must be referentially explicit in using language. The speaker must also clearly describe the principal activities of the characters/objects involved. In particular, a necessary convention in recounting a series of events is that any significant changes in characters, time or location must be mentioned by the speaker.

In extracts (3) and (4) below we see speakers coping successfully with these requirements.

(3) there's this man and <u>his wife</u> sitting in the living room + and <u>his wife</u> is reading a paper + and the man was bored so he got up and walked to the window + and <u>his wife</u> just looked at him + then he went away and got dressed + then started looking in the mirror + and <u>his wife</u> was still reading the paper + then he went to a pub and talked and talked to the barman + then after that he started dancing + then he met <u>this girl</u> + and they sat down and started talking and had a drink + after that the man went home and then + picked up the phone and

his wife was listening + and after that + his wife was crying and he started explaining to her + then he packed his suitcase and he + his wife was crying on the bed + and he moved in a house + with the + with the girl and the removal men come through the door with the bed + then they started watching television in the living room + man lying back with his feet up on a pouffe + and the girl was just lying about + doing nothing she was bored + then the girl started looking out the window + and the man never knew what to do + then the girl left him with a smile and the man was awfully sad + then the man's wife went to a party + and met this guy + and you saw the man walking down the stairs + with a sad and the girl with a sad face

In this example the speaker makes it fairly clear who is involved in the story. The characters are referred to in ways which make it reasonably easy for the hearer to distinguish which character was doing what at various points. Two female characters are involved, but the speaker refers to these potentially confusable characters in ways which allow the hearer to keep them distinct. The particular problem for the speaker is the points in the story when one or other of the female characters appears or reappears in the story at a moment when the hearer's attention has just been focussed on the other female character. We shall illustrate this problem.

In the pictures from which the speaker is telling the story, a female character is shown in pictures a – c. The speaker introduces this character as 'his wife' and uses the same expression in subsequent descriptions of this character. The speaker then goes on to concentrate on the male character's activities and the first female character is not mentioned again in the next few lines of the story. When the speaker comes to describe later events, a second female character has to be introduced in a way which will let the hearer know that this is indeed a different female character and not a reappearance of the previously mentioned one. This speaker describes the relevant events by saying that the man in the story 'met this girl' and again the speaker is consistent in later mentions of this character, consistently using the expression 'the girl'. When a pronoun is used, this only occurs where the alternative female character in the story has not been mentioned for some time. The speaker, by using very simple language consistently, has successfully coped with one of the main requirements of this kind of task.

If we now consider how well this speaker communicates to his hearer where and when the various events occur, we notice that this performance is also quite successful in these respects. The speaker indicates by using expressions such as 'then he went to a pub', and 'after that the man went home' when it is that relevant changes in time and/or place have occurred.

If we look at another performance, example (4), we see a speaker using rather different language to tackle the requirements of this task. In fact this speaker is not as consistent as the previous speaker in the descriptions used for the characters in the story. For example, the first female character is introduced as '<u>Mrs Smith</u>', but later in the story when this character reappears, the expression '<u>his wife</u>' is used. It seems unlikely that this change will cause the hearer any problems as 'Mr Smith' has been mentioned recently, and the only other female character in the story is described in the same sentence using a quite different expression, '<u>the young lady</u>'. The speaker also uses different descriptions to introduce and then, subsequently, to refer to this second female character but again the change from '<u>a young lady with long black hair</u>' to '<u>the young lady</u>' seems unlikely to present the hearer with problems of interpretation.

(4) one day Mr and <u>Mrs Smith</u> were sitting + in their living room + and deciding what to do + when + Mr Smith went to look out the window + he thought whether to go out or stay in and watch the usual + night TV + then Mr Smith said to himself + that he should go out and enjoy himself + so he went out + to the hall + with his usual suit and tie and there he was dancing with a <u>young lady with long black hair</u> + + after the song had finished they sat down together and had a drink or two + when the dance finished Mr Smith returned home and phoned <u>the young lady</u> while <u>his wife</u> was listening at the door + he went he went to meet <u>the lady</u> + and for a change <u>Mrs Smith</u> was sitting alone on a chair + wondering what to do + <u>she</u> was crying + and then went off to bed still crying while Mr Smith left the house with his luggage + + he went to meet <u>the lady</u> and got a new house + then just before bed they were relaxing watching TV + when <u>the young lady</u> looked out the window + and + later <u>she</u> decided to leave <u>she</u> went out and <u>Mrs Smith</u> was at the club dancing + but at the stairs Mr Smith and <u>the young lady</u> were there too + feeling very depressed

This performance shows that to communicate successfully about who is doing what in such a simple story (which we have called the need to be referentially explicit) does not necessarily require the speaker to be absolutely consistent in his use of expressions. The speaker only needs to be sufficiently consistent and sufficiently explicit to avoid confusing the hearer. How consistent or explicit 'sufficiently' consistent or explicit is, will depend on the particular task being performed. If a story involves a larger number of 'same-gender' characters, (i.e. of female or male characters or neuter objects) then the more potentially confusing any changes in expressions will become. Similarly, the type of 'dynamic' task will be relevant. If a speaker is for instance describing a car crash (see Figure 4a, Appendix A for a task of this type which we have used widely), then the descriptions of the cars involved must be very consistent to avoid confusing the hearer, because all the kinds of things the speaker is likely to say about one car, are equally likely to apply to another car.

In example (5) we will see how a speaker can make things very difficult for the hearer to understand if he fails to be *sufficiently* referentially explicit even in a fairly simple story:

(5) the lady was reading the letter + the man got up from his seat and went to the window + + aftet they had a discussion + he went the man went + to the mirror and fixed his tie + + he went out to a disco club and the man shook the barman's hand + they started dancing + after that they started talking + + after that they went home + and the man phones somewhere + he went through to the living room + and told the lady + the girl the lady started crying + he got a new house + + and he moved into it + the lady went up to the window + and then went outside + and then went to + a disco club

In this version of the story, the speaker introduces the first female character as 'the lady' and then refers to this character in conjunction with the male character by using the pronoun 'they'. When the speaker reintroduces the first female character, he again uses the expression 'the lady' so the hearer should have no difficulty understanding who 'was told' and 'started crying'.

At the point in the story where the speaker should introduce the distinct second female character, when 'dancing/talking' etc. is mentioned, this speaker unhelpfully again uses the pronoun 'they'. We can judge from the pictures, that the 'they' in question refers to the male character and the second female character, but from this speaker's description the hearer would not understand this, and indeed might assume that the man was dancing with the barman. The speaker has failed to be referentially explicit at this point in the story. When describing the later activities, he is forced to reintroduce the second female character. Again this speaker chooses to use the expression 'the lady', which is unhelpful for the hearer. The only 'lady' the hearer really knows about is the first mentioned female character, and so the hearer probably assumes that it is this character who has been reintroduced into the story.

This speaker, by two infelicitous choices of expression to refer to one character, has presented a story which the hearer is extremely unlikely to understand in the intended way. Instead of a story of marriage – boredom – unfaithfulness – new liaison – boredom, which most speakers describe, this particular story sounds like a rather aimless account of moving house. This version illustrates how a speaker's failure to be sufficiently referentially explicit can have serious consequences for adequate communication to a hearer. Further examples of the kind of problems speakers exhibit with this requirement will be discussed when we discuss how to assess talk in Chapter 5.

We have seen how the appearance and reappearance of characters or objects in 'dynamic' tasks highlights the need for referential explicitness. We have said that the other main requirement of special relevance to 'dynamic' tasks is that the speaker clearly indicates when spatial or temporal changes have occurred. In examples (3) and (4), the speakers were both quite helpful to the hearer in marking those points in the story where such changes occur. The hearers throughout those stories would be able to judge when the scene changed.

In contrast, the short extracts (6) and (7) below, show how potentially confusing the story can become when speakers fail to mark such shifts.

(6) the man and the lady are sitting down talking + the lady is reading a letter + the man is sitting smoking a cigarette + the lady sits down and the man looks out the window + the man goes to the window he gets dressed and goes to the window and makes himself smart + <u>the lady is still sitting there</u> + <u>with the letter</u>[1] + <u>the man shakes hands</u>[2] + <u>with his friend</u> + and meets a girl + and he starts dancing with her

(7) then he goes to this pub or cafe + has a pint + and he starts dancing with this woman + and he starts talking to the woman + <u>he starts to like her</u>[3] + <u>and the wife hears him phoning her on the phone</u>[4]

In these two extracts the speakers fail to indicate explicitly when a change of location has occurred in the story. As a result, the hearers could well misunderstand both where and when the various activities take place. For example, in (6), the story seems potentially confusing because the speaker does not mention that between event 1 and event 2, the man in the story has left home and gone to a dance. The story as it stands seems confusing because strange people, 'the friend' and 'a girl', and activities, 'dancing', seem to occur out of the blue, in the same location as 'sitting' and 'reading'.

In extract (7) the speaker fails to mention the change of location between events 3 and 4, i.e. that the man goes home: this is potentially misleading to the hearer because it disrupts the logical appearance and reappearance of the characters in the story. 'The wife' seems to appear in the pub suddenly. The failure to mark the change of location also upsets the temporal sequence of the story, in that the two events do not seem separated in time. In story (3), by the insertion of the simple phrase 'after that the man went home' between two events which are otherwise similarly described in the two versions, the temporal as well as the spatial organisation of the story is made perfectly clear.

We have concentrated in these examples on the way speakers cope with those requirements which are characteristic of tasks involving dynamic relationships, namely the need for referential explicitness and the need to indicate clearly changes in time and location.

However, as in 'static' tasks, a successful performance will also include an adequate amount of information concerning the actual details of the events shown in the stimulus material. In hundreds of recordings we have made of pupils telling a variety of stories, there are very few performances which are inadequate in terms of information content. Pupils produce performances which do vary in the amount of information provided, but virtually all pupils adequately describe the main events in a story. Therefore we have concentrated in this discussion on those features of story-telling which are also found in other tasks involving dynamic relationships, such as describing a car crash, or giving an eye witness account of a crime, which pupils often have problems with. If a teacher wishes to use a story-telling task, either to encourage or to assess the ability to transfer particular information, then by analysing the content of the stimulus material, either as a whole or in part, objective criteria can be drawn up describing information which a speaker should mention if a performance is to be judged successful. In Chapter 5, where assessment is discussed in more detail, we describe an exercise where teachers assessed the amount of information which speakers provided at the beginning of their stories. This illustrates one approach which teachers could adopt to encourage speakers to 'set the scene' adequately at the beginning of a story.

As we are mainly concerned with developing a structured syllabus, where the communicative tasks a pupil attempts can be placed in ascending order of difficulty, we shall concentrate our descriptions of each task and task type on those features which present speakers with problems rather than on those aspects of tasks which the vast majority accomplish with ease. This, of course, is not to under-value the speakers' achievements, but to concentrate the teachers' and the pupils' attention on those areas where help or practice is required before an adequate level of communicative competence can be achieved. It is clear that there is room for improvement in all speakers' performances in some aspects of some tasks. Even mature and highly educated speakers find it hard to transfer information adequately in some tasks such as giving an account of a car accident involving five cars manoeuvring at a crossroads.

4.1.4 Tasks involving abstract relations

We have seen how the simplest communicative tasks involve information about people or objects that are stable and we called such tasks 'static' tasks. 'Dynamic' tasks in which the speaker has to describe changing events and activities were found to be more difficult. In both these types of task, the stimulus material which we present to pupils contains all the information which has to be transferred to the hearer.

In contrast the tasks which involve the pupil himself giving an account of abstract relations are much more difficult for the teenage speakers we have worked with.

In such tasks, as when a speaker has to express an opinion on a given topic, or offer a justification for a particular action, although we provide identical stimulus material designed to elicit the expression of opinion or justification, the stimulus material does not contain the actual content to be communicated. If we consider in detail one 'abstract' task which we have used with many pupils, we can begin to see how the nature of such a task can present problems for many young speakers. In this task speakers are shown a short video film in which a Scottish schoolteacher delivers a one-minute speech in which he strongly supports the use of 'the belt' in schools. The text of this speech is given below.

We chose this stimulus material since it is a subject which pupils are familiar with, and which they might be expected to have their own views about.

Text of video film 'The Belt'

This is an instrument with which you will be entirely familiar. I can remember that when I was a boy, I was also quite familiar with it. I'm still quite familiar with it – from this end. But when I was a boy, this was the end I knew best. Now, you may well ask why it is necessary that the belt should still be used in Scottish schools. It is necessary because the teacher has to be in control. If the teacher is in control in the classroom, then proper attention will be paid to the lesson. When the pupils are paying attention to the teacher, then he can do what he is paid to do, which is to teach. After all, the teacher is in school to teach, and the pupils are there to be taught. This is what education is about, and without the belt, education will not take place.

Immediately after seeing the film, each pupil was asked 'What do you think about that?'. Further prompt questions were asked if the speaker seemed unsure of what was required. In all cases, if the speaker was unwilling or unable to produce an extended answer to the first question, he tended to continue to provide single word or brief phrase answers to all subsequent questions. All the responses which we discuss are therefore those given to the first standard question asked of all speakers.

What is it that is required of speakers in this task in terms of information to be communicated? The speaker must state whether he agrees or disagrees with what has been said and presumably a 'good' communicator would also include information to justify this expressed opinion. The information to be communicated then, is the speaker's evaluation or response to the stimulus material. It is not a simple repetition of the stimulus material. The speaker has to process a fairly large package of information, extract and summarise the basic message from this, decide or recall his own views on the subject, frame these views as a response to those stated on the film, select information to support this response either from past experience or from information on the film, and state this clearly. Not only is this a fairly long list of requirements, but the *speaker* also has to evaluate, select, and structure the information. In contrast, in 'static' and 'dynamic' tasks, the stimulus material itself provides all the content to be communicated, which means the selection of information and its structure are largely predetermined for the speaker.

4.1.5 Examples of speakers' performances on tasks involving abstract relations

Some examples for performances from an 'abstract' task will show how speakers cope with the task requirements.

(8) it's a man sitting behind a desk talking about + why belts are used in Scottish + Scottish schools + + he says that if the belt wasn't used + people pupils in the class wouldn't be taught + and that it is used because people in the class + don't eh pay much attention + while the teacher is talking + but when she has when the teacher has got a belt + everyone listens and learns more + and the teacher teaches them more and gets money for teaching them + and if the belt wasn't used + they wouldn't be taught in school as nobody pays attention in the class

(9) I don't think it's true

(10) I disagree with him cause there could be other means of punishing people

(11) the man was quite right + if you do something bad you're better
getting punished like that than getting anything else + that's over
and done with and so you get hit in the hand and it's sore for a wee
bit but and it goes away + + like you get lines it could take your
time at night and that + and if you get kept in after school + detention + take your time away and all

The speaker in (8) copes quite well with the first task requirement,
namely processing the information presented in the stimulus material. If
we compare the text of the film with this speaker's extract, we see that he
fairly accurately recalls and reproduces (or paraphrases) the main arguments presented on film. The speaker, however, fails to meet all the
other task requirements. In fact, what this speaker has done is *describe*
the stimulus material in the task fairly extensively, and perhaps because
this in itself is quite demanding, the speaker does not then attempt to go
on and recall his own views, formulate a response, etc. Although we
might suppose that part of the problem is that this speaker misinterprets
the initial instruction 'What do you think about that?', even subsequent
alternative questions failed to elicit a response from the speaker which
would meet the other task demands.

In the performance shown in (9), we see another speaker who only
meets some of the requirements necessary for a good performance on this
task. This speaker has apparently processed the stimulus material and
the task instructions appropriately, has recalled or decided his own views
on the subject, and produces a statement which is clearly an opinion and
a response to the material presented on the film. The response, however,
contains very little information: for example, it does not include any supporting evidence for the speaker's view, nor indeed is there clear evidence that the speaker correctly interprets the views expressed on film.
These performances show the difficulty that some young speakers find in
coping with all the requirements of this task.

A few young speakers, even from the less academically able groups, do
cope with all the demands that 'abstract' tasks present. The speakers in
(10) and (11) are both clearly expressing an opinion, which represents a
response to their own summary of the views presented on film. They are
both also presenting information to support their opinion, which either
explicitly as in (11), or implicitly as in (10), allows us to judge what these
speakers thought the views expressed on film were.

In (11), the speaker draws on his own knowledge of the subject area in
general, to provide supporting evidence for the particular views expres-

sed on film. This speaker also evaluates alternatives to the view expressed, again drawing on relevant information known to him but not presented in the task. Both of these strategies seem to be valuable ones and as we shall see in Chapter 5, when we consider assessing such performances, example (11) might represent one model for a good performance on this task. (Note we are talking simply of what it is that the task type requires, not in general terms about rhetorical ability, fluency, extended vocabulary, etc.)

4.2 The grid of tasks of ascending difficulty

We have described why 'static' tasks are the easiest type of task, namely because the information to be transferred is all presented to the speaker in the stimulus material for the task. To perform the task successfully, the speaker has only to describe explicitly the information in front of him in a simple linear sequence.

Within this 'easy' category of tasks, we can, of course, devise more difficult versions of particular tasks by increasing the amount of information which the speaker has to transfer or by making the relationships between items of information more complex. A diagram task which involves the speaker describing a few elements which are roughly similar in size and which are evenly spaced one below the other is easier to describe than a diagram involving more elements in a less regular array. If speakers have to describe spatial relationships which involve left and right, we found many pupils became confused or uncertain. Having to specify several different sizes and directions also increases the difficulty of such tasks for the speakers. (See Figures 1a, 1b, and 1c, Appendix A for examples of easy and more difficult versions of 'static' tasks.) In general, however, we believe, and have found from recording many pupils performing a variety of task types, that this category of tasks poses the fewest problems for the young speaker. 'Dynamic' tasks are, on the whole, more difficult because although the information to be transferred is again presented to the speaker, so both content and structure are predetermined, the nature of the structure of such tasks can present the speaker with problems, as we saw in Section 4.1.3. To perform 'dynamic' tasks successfully, the speaker has to describe the stimulus material fully, and to be sufficiently explicit, discriminating and consistent in his use of language, for the hearer to understand the described events.

Again, within this category, we have constructed and tested easy and more difficult tasks. The number of characters or objects involved, particularly the number of similar characters or objects, and the nature and number of changes in the relationships among these, all make 'dynamic' tasks more or less difficult for speakers. Thus a story which involves four female characters interacting, is more difficult to describe than one involving only one female and one male character. A story which involves several changes of scene, or flashbacks to earlier events in time, is more difficult than a story which occurs at a single time and location. A crash between a car and a lorry on a straight road is easier to describe than an accident involving four cars at a crossroads.

In Table 4.1, we illustrate schematically how tasks can be compared in terms of difficulty. In Chapter 5, we will discuss the diagnostic and summative assessment potential of such a grid.

Table 4.1 Tasks of ascending difficulty

Degree of difficulty

→

Static task		Dynamic task		Abstract task
Task A	Task B ⟶	Task G	Task H ⟶	Task L ⟶
e.g.	e.g.	e.g.	e.g.	e.g.
Diagram	Pegboard	Story	Car crash	Opinion

Degree of difficulty ↑

Many elements, relationships, characters, etc. (more difficult)

Few elements, relationships, etc. (less difficulty)

4.3 Purpose of talk: effects of purpose on difficulty

As we note from Table 4.1, 'abstract' tasks were more difficult than other types of tasks. We believe that there may be a number of reasons for this.

First, although such tasks provide the speaker with stimulus material on which to base his response, the information content and the way this is structured have to be determined by the speaker. The nature of the instructions for such tasks may also cause the speaker problems. In 'abstract' tasks, the speaker has to produce a response geared to a particular purpose. If asked for an opinion or a justification, the speaker has to focus a response quite precisely, by selecting and presenting information relevant to that particular task. Many responses which appear to be quite relevant in terms of talking on the same topic as the stimulus material must be strictly judged to be irrelevant in terms of what the pupil is asked to do in a particular task. It is in this sense that the *purpose* of a task may impose considerable communicative stress on a speaker.

In a task where the speaker has to instruct the hearer how to draw a diagram, the speaker may actually present the information as a series of instructions, for example 'draw a big black square in the middle of the page' or he may present a series of descriptive statements 'there's a wee red line at the top'. Teachers may wish to encourage the first kind of response as a more appropriate response to the task, but the hearer trying to draw the diagram would probably cope quite easily with either. Similarly, in a story-telling task, we might value and encourage performances which contain details about characters' motivations and other 'good' narrative information compared to a bald but accurate description of the stimulus pictures, but hearers could probably understand the events in the 'story' even in the latter case. In contrast, if the hearer's task is to judge whether a speaker is in favour of corporal punishment in schools, and the speaker only describes the film that has been shown as a stimulus for expression of his own opinion, then the difference between the speaker's response and the question posed in the task represents a more serious communicative failure. Many speakers have difficulties with tasks which involve such speaking for a precise purpose, even when the content to be communicated is a concrete description of events. The problem for these speakers lies in thoroughly understanding the purpose of the task.

4.4 The summary task

In the grid shown in Table 4.1, the tasks involved all exploit basic information-transferring skills. We have worked extensively with such tasks and as a result know the communicative problems which they present for speakers. As a result of such investigations we have been able to draw up objective criteria for assessing the adequacy of performances on these kinds of tasks. Examples of such assessment protocols are described in some detail in Chapter 5.

There are a number of spoken language tasks which we have experimented with, which do not fit neatly into this pattern of tasks of ascending and specifiable levels of difficulty. In this section, we describe two of these tasks. Although they do not draw on identical information-transferring skills to those already described, the problems which speakers have to overcome to complete them successfully seem to be related to those described earlier in this chapter. As the two tasks in question, the task of summarising and the task of co-operatively exchanging information with a partner, are also of potential educational interest, we include them although any conclusions drawn from these studies are more tentative than those derived from our basic grid of tasks.

In one task which we have used, pupils were asked to give a short summary of a story from cartoon pictures. The instructions to the pupils stressed that only the most important things were to be included in this short version of the story, and that they were to imagine that, if their story was written down, it would only be two or three lines long. In other words, to complete this task successfully, speakers had to study the stimulus pictures, decide what was happening in the story, select the most important features, condense a description of these, and frame this description in a few moments of speech. This task, like the 'abstract' task, demands talk which is focussed for a particular purpose.

We found that most of our young speakers had considerable difficulties with this task. Many speakers appeared to have problems in tailoring their talk, even in terms of length, to the task they were asked to perform. Although not under any time pressure, and in spite of instructions to study the stimulus pictures carefully before beginning, many speakers spent little time in looking at the pictures before beginning to speak. This lack of time spent in consideration of the various events shown in the pictures, suggests that speakers had not weighed the relative importance of the events or made a careful selection of those to be included in their summary. The speakers also seemed over-dependent on the stimulus pictures. Although they might describe the first one or two pictures briefly, they seemed to forget or ignore the instructions to be brief and selective as they looked at later pictures, and included as much information in describing the later events, picture by picture, as was generally found when speakers were asked to tell the whole story.

As a result of these difficulties, speakers in this task tended to produce 'summaries' which were on average at least three times the required length, and in some cases, just as long as when the same speaker was asked to tell the whole story.

In recent research in the United States on summarising skills among school pupils, college students, and university postgraduate students, a hierarchy of skills has been described (Brown & Day, 1983). All of this research has concerned the production of written summaries of written texts. The most basic skill involved is the deletion of unimportant or redundant information, and in summarising simple texts even 10 year-olds were able to do this very effectively. The next skill, or summarising rule, which pupils and students learn to apply is that of 'superordination', where a more general term is applied to describe a list of particular items or a detailed description of particular actions. For example, if a text contained the sentence 'Daisies, poppies, marigolds and lilies stay in the form of seeds . . .', the person writing a summary of the text could substitute 'flowers' for the list of examples. This ability is less common in younger pupils, but 15 year-olds and older students can apply this effectively, at least in simple texts. The two skills which are more typical of more mature summarisers, are (a) selecting or inventing a topic sentence for the summary, which less than half the 15 year-olds were found to do, and (b) combining information from different parts of the story which was characteristic of, and largely limited to, the postgraduate population. Comments made by mature summarisers during the task showed how they used these two skills. Concerning the selection of a topic sentence for the summary one subject said, 'The paragraph is about the cycle of the annual plants that produce seeds, wait until rainfall, bloom, produce seeds again, etc. Although it doesn't say so explicitly, all you need is to state this cycle then you can drop the rest'. Older subjects also commented on how they combined information from different parts of the original text in their summaries. For example, one subject is quoted saying 'In the first two paragraphs the only really essential information is the facts about the heat and lack of water in the desert. I'll combine the first two paragraphs into only two sentences – that contains all the information that I need'.

4.4.1 Examples of performances on summarising and story-telling tasks

If we compare two pairs of performances on these two tasks we can see which rules or skills our speakers typically use or fail to use when producing spoken summaries. First each speaker recounts the story and then he produces a summary.

(12a) *Story*

there was a man and a lady they were sitting in a chair + in their house + the man got up and looked out the window + the lady stopped reading and watched him + + he got he went out the door + and got himself + smartly dressed + he fixed his tie in the mirror + + then he went to this club dance + he shook he shook hands with the barman + with his hands in his pocket + they were all dancing + the man met another woman he started to dance with her then they sat down + at a table + drinking together + he was

on the he was back home + + he was on the phone the woman
came in the door + heard him + the man tried to explain to her +
she was crying + she went to her bedroom she was still crying +
more now he went out the door with his suitcase + packed + and
he met the other woman in another house + the removal men were
bringing in all the furniture + + they were + on the couch together watching TV + the woman the other woman got up + and
looked out the window + she went out + he followed her + he shut
the door + think they went to a party + everyone was dancing

(12b) *Summary*

the man gets up and looks out his window + he's he's out the room
now + and he's fixing his tie in a mirror + the lady is still reading
+ he's at the club + he's shaking hands with the barman + he
starts to dance with a + different lady + they are drinking together
+ he is on the phone + they are in a different room + she starts
crying she is in her bedroom now + she is crying even more + + he
goes out the door with his suitcase + he is with the other woman
now + the removal men are bringing in all the parcels and + furniture + they are on the couch + he is watching telly + but she isn't
+ she looks out the window + she's got a cigarette in her mouth +
she goes out and the man follows + with a cigarette in his mouth +
and a jacket + they are at the club again

(13a) *Story*

starts with there is a man and a woman sitting in the living room +
the man was bored + so he + walked up and he was looking out the
window + + then he got + dressed + and he went out to a disco +
where he met a barman and he was having a real good time when he
met a girl + + and they started speaking + then the next night he
was on the phone to her and his wife heard him + and she started to
cry + then the wife was lying on the bed greeting her eyes out +
and the guy left her + and moved in with the young girl in a brand
new house + + the man the man was quite happy and girl was fed
up + then they're watching telly and she walks across and was
looking out the window + pretty bored + there well she says 'let's
go to the disco' and they went out + + the man was pretty bored +
and there he saw his wife having a good time with a young man

(13b) *Summary*

he was getting ready to go out + and he went to a disco + there he
met a girl + and the next night he was phoning her + + and his

wife found out + then + he moved in with the young girl + and he
was very happy but the young girl the young girl was very sad

The performance of the speaker in (12a) and (12b) is fairly typical of our
population. The story which was told early in the recording session
shows that the speaker understands the events shown in the stimulus pictures. In fact, using the criteria described in Section 4.1.2 this is a reasonably successful performance of story-telling. Thus any problems which
arise in the summarising task are likely to be due to the nature of that particular task and not to the stimulus material used.

The performance in (12b) is not a very successful one. Our first impression is that the speaker just says far too much for a 'three-line summary'.
However, within this performance we can see evidence both for the summarising skills described by Brown and Day, and for our own general descriptions of speakers' behaviour on this task.

If we examine the events described in story and summary, up to the
point when the main character is 'at the club', we see that in the story
these events take roughly twice as long to describe as in the summary. In
the summary, there is evidence that the speaker is deleting unimportant
details, for example by omitting to mention 'sitting in chairs' or 'went out
the door'. The speaker does not actually introduce the first female
character at the beginning of the story but does retain a description of the
man fixing his tie, so we might suggest that at the beginning of the summary, the speaker is applying a 'deletion of unimportant detail' rule, but
that this is not applied consistently and that some of the selection deci-
sions are rather erratic.

Later in the summary, this deletion rule seems to be applied less often
and more erratically. Not only is very trivial detail included in the summary, such as mentioning on two separate occasions when characters are
smoking, but some of this very unimportant information which is
included in the summary was not mentioned when the speaker earlier
told the complete story.

This speaker is not effective at selecting only the important information to include in a summary, and he is also poor at framing the information which he does choose to include, in a concise form of language. The
speaker generally uses the same linguistic forms in the summary as in the
story, so there is no evidence for a superordination rule (where a more
general term is substituted for a lengthier list of particulars).

In contrast to the inadequate summary shown in (12b), the speaker in
(13b) produces a performance which, at least in terms of length,
approaches the task requirements. If we compare this to the speaker's

original description of the stimulus material in the complete story, we note that this speaker much more effectively and consistently deletes unimportant details from the summary. This performance was one of a small number which approached the required length for this task. As in (12b) the only strategy of those described by Brown and Day, which even these more successful speakers employed in this task, was that of deletion of unimportant details.

In Chapter 6, we will describe how we attempted to elicit more successful summarising performances by manipulating the task stimuli and the conditions under which the task was performed.

The main point we wish to draw attention to here is that the purpose of the talk that a speaker is asked to produce greatly affects the ease or difficulty of the task for many young speakers.

4.5 Co-operative tasks

So far we have been largely concerned with conditions where one speaker is the authoritative speaker, supposed to transfer information to another pupil who plays a fairly passive role. It is this type of task which we have most experience of, which we are able to grade with some confidence, and which we provide assessment procedures for.

There are clearly other types of task which make rather different demands on speakers, but which may have other drawbacks like being much harder to grade or to assess.

One such task, which is very popular with pupils, is where the information required to complete a task is distributed between two pupils and they have to co-operate to complete the task. Thus speaker A may have in front of him a map of an island containing a number of dangerous features with a safe route marked across it. Speaker B may have a map of the same island but one said to be 'made by an earlier explorer' which contains some of the features on A's map, but not all, and contains, in addition, three features which are not marked on A's map. A is asked to describe to B the safe route across the island so that B can draw it in on his map.

The reason a task like this is difficult to grade or to assess is because the behaviour of one member of the pair depends so much on the behaviour of the other member. Coping with incompatible information is difficult for any of us – we all need to construct a coherent representation. Speakers taking the A role, the authoritative role (i.e. knowing the route) can be more or less helpful in response to the announcement by another speaker that his information is different. Consider the behaviour of the speakers taking the A role in the following examples (14) and (15):

(14) A: draw a line from the start and do it round the beach + tree + + Palm Beach and do it round the swamp and round the waterfall

 B: there is no swamp

 A: well there is one on mine + well just draw a line round the waterfall

(15) A: go a bit further upwards and you'll come to a bridge

 B: I haven't got a bridge

 A: oh well + where it says 'Big River' + go along a bit and draw a bridge in

In the first of these extracts, the speaker makes no attempt to accommodate B's information – merely reiterates her own. In the second, the speaker takes on B's incompatible information and instructs him to draw in the bridge which he hasn't got. This suggests one way of grading co-operative behaviour, which is to value highly an attempt to help the other speaker out when he has incompatible information, and to value less highly a mere reiteration of the speaker's own information. We could then suggest valuing least highly of all behaviour when the speaker simply ignores B's problem as in (16):

(16) A: go past the pine trees + past the swamp + and past the waterfall

 B: where's the swamp?

 A: then past the mountain and a bridge

Where B responds in an appropriate manner, then we can usefully talk about A's behaviour. However B does not always respond in an appropriate manner:

(17) A: go over the Big River + over a bridge

 B: done it

In (17) B responds 'done it' in spite of the fact that she has no bridge on her map. Where B speakers take a passive role, A speakers have no opportunity to demonstrate whether or not they are capable of taking account of the other speaker's state of knowledge and framing a helpful reply.

 It's perfectly possible to create a series of more or less difficult tasks using this format. The task will be simpler if (a) there are fewer rather than more incompatible features and (b) if the incompatibility lies in one speaker having a feature that the other lacks (e.g. B doesn't have the bridge over the river which A has) rather than two conflicting features in the same location (e.g. B has crocodiles where A has a swamp).

In spite of the difficulty of grading or assessing the task as it is actually performed, it still seems worthwhile including tasks of this sort in the teaching programme, precisely in order to give pupils practice in coping in a sympathetic and helpful way when the other speaker has incompatible information. Conversely, it also gives the pupil who takes the role of speaker B practice in taking on incompatible information and assimilating it to his view of the map. Consider the behaviour of B speakers in the following extracts:

(18) A: go to your left + just about come to the swamp
      B: where's the swamp + how far along?
(19) A: go over to quite a bit below the bottom of the swamp
      B: what swamp?
      A: swamp swamp
      B: how far is it away from Palm Beach?
(20) A: and across the bridge at Big River
      B: what bridge at Big River? +++ wait a minute + where's your bridge?

In each case the B speaker does not have the mentioned feature on his/her map. However, in each case they accommodate themselves to this new information and ask for the location of the feature. This is obviously going to be a more useful strategy than that employed by some pupils who simply state 'I've not got a swamp/bridge', leaving A to do all the work of telling them to draw it in.

This type of co-operative task does not, typically, give practice in long turns. What it does give practice in is transferring information in what the speaker may well have planned as a long turn, but what turns out to be a turn in which, in most cases, he keeps on getting interrupted because the listener needs to ask a question or check that he's understood. The ability to maintain a plan, and simultaneously cope with problems that the listener has, demands a considerable level of sophistication. Some of our population showed themselves to be sensitive and considerate speakers for at least some of the time. For others, the ability to perform under such circumstances obviously created considerable difficulty.

In Chapter 5, we describe the principles underlying the assessment procedures we have devised for the basic grid of tasks with detailed examples of scoring protocols for these tasks. Suggestions are also made about how teachers might go about objectively assessing performances of non-grid tasks.

5 Assessment

5.1 Choosing criteria

Being asked to judge how well a school pupil speaks is a daunting task. It might seem fairly straightforward to make a short judgment, along the lines of 'He speaks well, but lacks confidence: 70%'. The usefulness of such an assessment is questionable, to say the least. Imagine the task multiplied by 30, when a whole class is being assessed. What would it mean to say that one pupil had earned a 'score' of 70% and another a score of 50%? Would it mean that one of them was speaking differently in some clearly definable way, using different skills or using the same skills more effectively? Would it make any sense to compare them? Now multiply the task by 15, for instance, for the number of times any one pupil might be assessed during his secondary school career. Would it be possible to specify improvements in a pupil's spoken language skills over the course of a term, a year, two years? Is it even possible to keep in mind an individual's speaking skills from one year to the next so as to be able to make such a judgment? Does an individual necessarily improve from one year to the next? How closely are different teachers' judgments about the same pupil going to agree? What about a child who has never said anything in class?

More concretely, if concerned parents inquire about a pupil's assessment, how are they to be answered? If it was a low mark for mathematics, or even for written English, then it would be very straightforward to explain how the assessment was reached, to point to poor performance in term work or in exams; the responsibilities of the pupils, the school and the parents would be relatively clear-cut. Is there any way that we can extend to spoken language skills any kind of objective assessment?

In order to supply a means of objective assessment, we require a principled set of clear criteria.

The following two short studies were run in order (a) to investigate exactly what happens when a group of teachers assess the speech of a small group of pupils, and (b) to see if it is feasible to put into practice the type of assessment which we are advocating in this book.

5.2 Teachers using assessment criteria: the first study

Thirty teachers and student teachers were asked to make judgments about the speech of ten pupils on the basis of short tape recordings.

Five of the pupils were giving instructions for the diagram-drawing task, described in Chapter 4, and the other five were giving an account of a short public information-type video film which they had just seen. (The film was a cautionary story which showed a thief stealing from parked cars while a nearby crowd was watching a street performance of an escapologist.) In both cases, the amount of speech which each pupil produced was relatively small – lasting for only 60 seconds or less.

The judges were told that they would be scoring the speakers' performances in different ways. (Details are given in Appendix B.) We can call the first method 'unstructured scoring'; they were told to use whatever criteria they thought were appropriate in order to arrive at a score out of ten. The second method, 'structured scoring', involved a detailed scoring protocol – different for each of the two tasks – on which they were required to award a mark for specific pieces of information being clearly and unambiguously expressed in the speaker's account; the judges were told to concentrate on the informational content ('who did what') and not to award marks for specific vocabulary. (The term 'scoring protocol' is used to refer to the score sheet which bears the scoring procedure.)

We hoped, in this way, to demonstrate that teachers are able to use a structured scoring procedure to produce consistent results; it remained to be seen how these assessments would compare with their own judgments using their own personal, impressionistic criteria.

The teachers were divided into two groups. The first group judged the stories, using unstructured scoring, and then the diagram instructions, using structured scoring. This was reversed in the case of the second group, who judged diagram instructions using unstructured assessment and then stories using structured assessment.

Details of the results are given in Appendix C. We found that the teachers' assessments were very consistent in all conditions. Regardless of the details of the assessment there was always a clear consensus as to how the performances should be ranked. More surprisingly, the two methods of assessment produced different rankings, as seen below, in the judgments of the story-telling performances.

	Structured scoring		*Unstructured scoring*
Speaker number	3	'best' performance	2★
	4		5★
	1		3
	2★		4
	5★	'worst' performance	1

For the purposes of this study, we selected three performances from academically less able pupils which were good performances in terms of information content, and two performances from academically more able pupils which were relatively poor performances in informational terms. The two academically more able speakers, numbers 2 and 5, are asterisked above.

A similar pattern emerged in the judgments of the diagram descriptions; one academically less able speaker and one academically more able speaker swapped between first and third place in the rankings for structured versus unstructured assessments, with the structured assessment favouring the academically less able speaker.

This crossover – with the rankings of the two types of speaker being more or less reversed – means that different criteria are being used in the two assessment procedures. We know that the criteria in the structured scoring were those of information content; the judges assessed how successful the performance was as a piece of transactional (information-related) speech. What were the criteria being used when it was left to the teachers themselves to choose their own? We asked them to comment afterwards on how they thought they were arriving at their judgments in the unstructured condition. Their answers differed widely; often they were trying to concentrate on information content, 'identification of the main characters in the story', 'detail and precision', in the case of the story, 'colours, distances . . . and dimensions', in the diagram descriptions; often, though, much more impressionistic and unquantifiable criteria were used, such as 'the clearest speaker', 'good pronunciation', 'fluency', use of 'sort of', and 'vocabulary'. Nevertheless, there was still a good consensus among them as to how the performances should be ranked.

This short study shows, then, that it is possible for teachers to reach a reliable consensus about the relative abilities of a group of school pupils based on a relatively brief tape recording of performance in a verbal task. The study also shows that academically less able speakers' skills in purely transactional speech tend to be under-valued unless the scoring procedure is deliberately structured so as to exclude the non-transactional skills from the assessment. This is not to devalue those other aspects of performance such as fluency, clarity, vocabulary, confidence, and so on; these clearly affect the impression gained by a listener and are probably very important in situations such as interviews. What is more, the teachers seemed to agree substantially when left to determine their own criteria, suggesting that it might be worthwhile trying to fix these other criteria – such as fluency, clarity, coherence, and so on – even if only for the purpose of excluding such judgments from the assessment of transactional speech.

This study demonstrated that teachers are able to make consistent judgments on the information content of speech, once the details of that content are drawn to their attention. Clearly, this is crucial to the approach which we are suggesting.

5.3 Teachers using assessment criteria: the second study

The second study employed thirty principal teachers of English as judges. They were given an assessment booklet (see Appendix B) together with a cassette recording of school pupils performing in three different tasks. The assessment exercise breaks down into three parts, which are considered in turn, below.

5.3.1 Teachers assessing descriptions of car crashes
A full description of the car crash task is to be found in Appendix A. The speaker's task involved giving an 'eye witness acount' of a car crash, presented by means of a series of photographs. The judges were given five such performances to listen to, four of them from academically more able pupils and one from an academically less able pupil. The performances ranged between 75 and 135 words; the judges were asked to listen to the performances twice.

The assessment consisted of making three judgments for each performance of the configuration of cars at the beginning, middle and end of the crash. As Appendix B shows, each judgment involved simply ticking one of three possible configurations given on the sheet; if the description was completely unclear, then a 'don't know' box would be ticked.

The judges were asked not to spend more than 15 minutes on the exercise. Details of the results are given in Appendix C. They show that the teachers were making similar judgments about the speech they were hearing; there was a significant consensus on 12 out of the 15 judgments they were asked to make. In the case of the first speaker they heard, for instance, they were in clear agreement about what that speaker was saying, about the information content of that speaker's performance; the speaker was describing a scene like x, then a scene like y, and then a scene like z.

These results mean that this assessment procedure is one way in which teachers can reach an agreed scoring of a pupil's performance in a task demanding transactional communication.

As analysts, we have privileged knowledge of the state of affairs which the speaker was trying to describe; the stimulus materials were even designed with a view to the particular difficulties of description which they would present to a speaker. In this way, it is possible for us to say that there is a 'correct' choice of pictures for the beginning, middle and end of the crash. One out of the three configurations of cars for the beginning of the crash is the 'correct' description, in that we know that it is modelled on the stimulus materials which the speaker is trying to describe, and likewise for the three possible configurations for the middle and end of the crash. It is only in this sense that we can say that a pupil's description was satisfactory or 'correct'; the teachers in our study did not have any such knowledge of the stimulus materials which prompted the speaker's description.

5.3.2 Teachers assessing narrative descriptions
After assessing the car crash descriptions, the judges were required to listen to six very short excerpts from pupils' performances in a story-telling task. (This task is discussed at more length in Chapter 4.) The pupils were required to tell a story, as if to a friend, the story being presented to them in the form of a series of line drawings. For the purposes of this assessment task, only the beginnings of the pupils' stories were presented to the judges; they were asked to score the stories by putting ticks against a checklist of details taken from the first two pictures of the cartoon story.

An analysis of the scores which the judges gave to the six speakers showed that they were marking the performances in a highly consistent way. The ranking of the performances, from 'adequate' to 'least adequate' was very similar for each of the judges; details of the results are given in Appendix C.

5.3.3. Teachers assessing expressions of opinion
The third task which this set of judges was required to assess was the opinion-expressing task described in Chapter 4. The judges were given recordings of the performance of six pupils together with the scoring protocol included in Appendix B. The judges were told that the total time for them to assess all six performances should not exceed 15 minutes – a practical amount of time, in terms of assessing a whole class.

The judges rated each of the performances as a Grade A, B or C performance as defined on the scoring protocol. The simple guidelines are repeated below.

Grade A: opinion expressed
        plus a reason given
        plus an alternative considered

Grade B: opinion expressed
          plus a reason given
          but *no* alternative considered
Grade C: opinion expressed
          but *no* reason given
          and *no* alternative considered

The performances which were selected for this exercise were intended to be representative of all the types of performance which our criteria defined: two were typical of Grade A, two were typical of Grade B, one was typical of Grade C and one was the type of null response which we found twice in 38 performances and which we judged did not merit being awarded a Grade C.

The judges agreed with our own predetermined assessments, unanimously in half of the cases. For the Grade A performances there was 80% and 87% agreement, respectively; for the Grade B performances there was 100% agreement in both instances; for the Grade C performance there was 100% agreement; for the 'unclassifiable' performance there was 83% agreement.

These assessment studies – using both student teachers and very experienced teachers – show that it is perfectly feasible to assess transactional speech, using criteria which are motivated by theory and which can be clearly stated. This means that it is not only possible to produce an overall 'mark' for a pupil, indicating general progress in transactional speech, but it is also possible to identify specific areas of difficulty. The studies just described have also demonstrated the objectivity of this approach to assessment; substantially the same results would be obtained for a particular pupil at a particular time no matter which teacher in the English Department was responsible for the testing. The pupil's progress could still be charted even though responsibility for the pupil moved from one English teacher to another.

5.4 Reasons for creating each pupil's taped record

In the assessment studies just described, teachers were given a tape of the pupils' performances and it was from these tapes that the teachers worked. Some people may ask if this is really necessary – scoring a pupil's performance as it is being given, there and then, would surely save time and effort. The answer to this is that there are several important reasons why it is preferable to create a taped record of each pupil's performance.

First, in tasks involving quite complex descriptions – the descriptions of car crashes, for instance – it is often necessary to listen to a performance more than once in order to score it accurately. This is particularly the case if the teacher is having difficulty with the speaker's accent, or if the description is fragmentary – for whatever reason. If the teacher is not prepared to put in the required amount of extra effort to interpret this kind of performance, then the whole enterprise will be jeopardised; the teacher will not be assessing simple information content, it will be the mixture-as-before of information content plus clarity plus fluency plus confidence. As the first study of teachers' assessment showed, it would mean that the skills of the academically less able pupils would be likely to be under-valued. A taped record is necessary if pupils' performances are to be accurately assessed. It might be added that it is considerably easier to restrict judgments to the information content of the performance if it is taped. Listening to a 'live' performance, and trying to assess it at the same time, makes it impossible to avoid registering impressions which are irrelevant as far as the scoring of the transfer of information is concerned. Eye-contact, gesture, facial expression and so forth all distract the listener's attention.

A second argument for creating a taped record is that situations will invariably arise where it is desired that pupils' performances can be listened to by other members of the English Department, or by an external assessor, in order to diagnose the specific problems a particular pupil is having. It may also be necessary to return to a pupil's past performance in order to demonstrate progress.

5.5 Realistic procedures in scoring from tapes

A complete transcription of a pupil's performance is an advantage in almost any assessment of a spoken performance. This is an ideal solution which must be ruled out in most cases, though, as transcribing from a tape is an extremely time-consuming business. The advantage in scoring and assessing transcribed performances is that a performance can be read faster than it can be listened to, and specific points in the performance can be found or returned to more rapidly; transcripts also offer an inexpensive means of retaining a record of past performances, and are a convenient medium for external moderation.

Later in this chapter, when examples are given of ways of scoring particular types of task, it will be seen that some types of task will reward a complete transcription much more than others. In some tasks, where assessment consists of giving marks simply for the mention of specific details, little is accomplished by transcribing the performance; it may be scored just as accurately and informatively by listening to the tape twice, perhaps three times at the most. In other tasks, assessment may consist of consistently making reference back to information which the pupil has given at previous points in the performance; in this case, it may well be worthwhile transcribing the tape as it means that more can be learned about the pupil's performance.

It should be remembered that consistent assessments were obtained from the teachers in the two studies described earlier, when the performances they were listening to were only one or two minutes long. It will place things in perspective if the time taken to assess spoken English is compared with the time taken to assess written English; if the teaching of spoken English is to be a highly-valued part of the syllabus, like written English, then a commensurate amount of time and effort should be given over to its assessment.

The scoring of different types of task

We shall now consider examples of types of task which we have employed and demonstrate the precise scoring procedures which have been evolved.

Scoring the 'static' tasks

The following two tasks present fewest problems for the speaker; they involve the description of static configurations.

5.6 Scoring the diagram-drawing task

Figure 1a in Appendix A shows one of the simple line diagrams which speakers were asked to describe.

Below are two speakers' instructions, each of them speaking to a partner who was waiting with a blank sheet of paper, a black pen and a red pen.

(1) Speaker 1: Draw a black square + + underneath it draw a red line + the same size + as the bottom line of the square + underneath it + and a small line up above it + on the right-hand side + and up above the red square + a number three

(2) Speaker 2: You draw a square + + + in the right hand at the bottom of the square + a little bit down there's a red line + same length as your square + + then at the top + a bit a bit larger space than the bottom + another red line but not as big as the other one + about half the size + + done it + + where that red line is at the top you draw a three

In Table 5.1 there is a scoring protocol for this particular diagram. It consists of a list of the entities in the diagram, their essential properties (colour and size) and their location. It is all the information which the listener requires to draw a reasonably adequate version of the diagram. (The examples given merely illustrate the range of acceptable possibilities.)

Table 5.1 Scoring protocol for the diagram-drawing task

Item	Examples of adequate expressions	Speaker 1	Speaker 2
Square	'a square', 'a box'	1	1
Colour	'black'	1	0
Size	'medium size square', 'about 5 cms square'	0	0
Direction	'on the right-hand side of your paper'	0	0
Distance	'at the top of the right-hand side'	0	0
Line 1	'a line'	1	1
Colour	'red'	1	1
Size	'double the length of the other line', 'same length as the square'	1	1
Direction	'underneath that'	1	1
Distance	'about 1cm', 'a little underneath'	0	1
Line 2	'a line'	1	1
Colour	'red'	0	1
Size	'small', 'just enough to cover the bottom of your three'	1	1
Direction	'up above it', 'above the square'	1	1
Distance	'about 2 cm away from', 'a wee bit underneath'	0	1
Figure 3	'a three', 'a wee line . . . a line diagonal + then a wee round circle + half circle'	1	1
Colour	'black'	0	0
Size	'quite large', 'big . . . the same size'	0	0
Direction	'above it', 'in your right-hand corner'	1	1
Distance	'about a cm above that', 'just down a wee bit	0	1
	Total score:	11	14

The examples are taken from both academically more able and less able pupils performing on this same task; the scores for Speakers 1 and 2 have been included.

The same score is given for the reply 'about a centimetre above that' and the reply 'just down a wee bit', even though the first is more accurate in absolute terms. This is an important principle. The reason behind this is that we are interested in assessing the ability to transfer information and not the ability to make precise spatial judgments. For a pupil to score maximum points in this task, it must be clear from the instructions to the listener that the pupil recognises the need to mention all of the discrete entities in the diagram. The pupil must also at least attempt to fill all of the 'information slots' associated with each separate entity – colour, size, direction and distance, in this case; whether these slots are filled stylishly, or with mathematical precision does not matter for the particular type of assessment we discuss here. If the purposes of our assessment were different, then the precision of the spatial judgments might become an element which could be scored, just as we might wish to score for a rich vocabulary for other reasons. Our present purpose, though, is simply to score the recognition of the need to supply certain information.

It will be clear that there is nothing absolute about the information we have chosen to score, the 'information slots' of colour, size and so on. The only way to judge the importance of these categories, and hence their relevance to our scoring protocol, is to give the task to pupils and discover how their responses differ and how their listeners interpret the instructions to draw the diagram. For instance, to take an extreme case, it would not tell us anything about the pupils' abilities if maximum points could only be earned by describing a line as 'a straight line of normal pencil thickness and of constant thickness'; such things are taken for granted in drawing a line in a diagram and no one bothers to mention them, except in relation to diagrams in which there are indeed lines of different thicknesses, dashed lines and so on. It also seems that the default orientation of a line in a diagram is 'horizontal'. From the analysis of the performances of 14–16 year-olds on this task, though, the elements in Table 5.1 appear to be central to an adequate set of instructions to draw the figure, at least for that age group.

The total scores enable us to say that Speaker 2 produced the more adequate description. Note that in this simple scoring procedure no one piece of information has been thought any more important than any other. There has been no weighting of the marks. The pieces of information have all been allocated one mark each. Note also that there is no particular route which the speaker should take in giving the description; it does not matter whether the description begins with the square, the figure 'three' or the lines. In certain tasks, though, there are distinct advantages in providing speakers with a point from which to begin their description, a 'start'. This makes different performances more comparable and makes the descriptive task somewhat easier insofar as it provides some elementary structure for the description. It is perhaps comparable with the way in which speakers in 'dynamic' tasks usually choose to begin their descriptions with the earliest point in time, in the series of events they are describing.

5.7 Scoring the pegboard task

Figure 2a, in Appendix A, shows one of the pegboard configurations which speakers were asked to describe. Below are two examples of a speaker giving instructions to a partner who was waiting with a blank pegboard and a collection of pegs and elastic bands.

(3) Speaker 1: Halfway to the pegboard + + put a red + peg + and + + just to the right-hand side + + put a yellow + + then ummm + down umm put a red peg again + + and join with a green elastic band + + slightly below it + but beside it + put + a blue peg + + after you've done that put a blue peg at the + right-hand + side + + halfway + + and then + a red peg down below it + + and then beside it + put a blue peg + + and join it with a red elastic band

(4) Speaker 2: On the bottom of the pegboard + right-hand side put a red peg in + + and then about a couple of + a wee while a wee bit up put a blue peg in + + and then across from the red peg + a wee drop a wee bit + put a blue peg in + + and then put a red elastic band round it + + then from the blue + from the blue opposite the red + + halfway about halfway up the page + put a red peg in + + and then a wee bit up above that put a yellow peg in + + then across from the yellow peg + on your left + put a red peg in + then put a green elastic band round it + + and then down from your red + opposite your yellow + and opposite the red put a blue peg in

Table 5.2 is a scoring protocol for this particular pegboard configuration; as can be seen, it closely resembles the way in which the diagram-drawing instructions were scored. One mark is allocated for each item of required information in the description.

The quotations given as examples are taken from Speakers 1 and 2; the numbers of the pegs are given in Figure 2a. (The speakers did not see the numbers.) A speaker scored one mark for mentioning the *colour* of a peg and three marks respectively for mentioning the *distance* and *direction* of the peg being described from a *fixed reference point*. One mark was scored for mentioning in the instructions to the listener the colour of an elastic band, and then another mark was scored for giving the *location* of the band.

Taking Speaker 1's instructions for placing Peg 1, the listener hears 'Halfway to the pegboard + + put a red + peg'; one mark is awarded for giving the colour, 'red', one mark is awarded for giving a reference point by which the peg's position can be described (in this case, 'the pegboard' has been interpreted as a reference point), and one mark is awarded for giving some idea of distance away from the reference point. Speaker 1 fails to give any idea of direction; 'halfway . . . on the right' would have been much more informative.

In comparison, Speaker 2 gives the following instructions concerning Peg 1: '+ + then across from the yellow peg + on your left + put a red peg in + '. This instruction, like Speaker 1's, mentions colour and a re-ference point, the yellow peg, but it differs in that there is information about direction but not about distance; the listener knows that the red peg belongs across to the left of the yellow peg, but has not been told how far to the left. Speaker 2 therefore scores on Direction but not on Distance.

Table 5.2 Scoring protocol for the pegboard task

Item	Examples of adequate expressions	Speaker 1	Speaker 2
Peg 1			
Colour	'red'	1	1
Reference point	'the pegboard', 'the yellow peg'	1	1
Direction	'on your left'	0	1
Distance	'halfway'	1	0
Peg 2			
Colour	'yellow'	1	1
Reference point	'a red peg'	1	1
Direction	'to the right-hand side', 'up above that'	1	1
Distance	'just', 'a wee bit'	1	1
Peg 3			
Colour	'blue'	1	1
Reference point	'it' (green band?), 'your red . . . your yellow . . . the red'	1	1
Direction	'below', 'down from . . . opposite your . . . opposite the'	1	1
Distance	'slightly'	1	1

Item	Examples of adequate expressions	Speaker 1	Speaker 2
Peg 4			
Colour	'red'	1	1
Reference point	'a yellow', 'the blue opposite the red'	1	1
Direction	'down', 'up the page'	1	1
Distance	'halfway about halfway'	0	1
Band 1			
Colour	'green'	1	1
Location	'and join with a green elastic band', 'then put a green elastic band round it'	1	1
Peg 5			
Colour	'blue'	1	1
Reference point	(the pegboard?), 'the red peg'	1	1
Direction	'the right-hand side', 'up'	1	1
Distance	'halfway', 'about a couple of . . . a wee while a wee bit up'	1	1
Peg 6			
Colour	'blue'	1	1
Reference point	'a red peg . . . it', 'the red peg'	1	1
Direction	'across from'	0	1
Distance	'beside it', 'a wee drop a wee bit'	1	1
Peg 7			
Colour	'red'	1	1
Reference point	'a blue peg', 'the pegboard'	1	1
Direction	'down below it', 'right-hand side'	1	1
Distance	'on the bottom'	0	1
Band 2			
Colour	'red'	1	1
Location	'join it with a red elastic band', 'put a red elastic band round it'	1	1
	Total score	28	31

The reader may care to work through the rest of the two performances, checking the marks allotted in Table 5.2. It will soon be seen that even with such a strictly 'objective' scoring procedure, instances arise which are marginal and call for the speaker to be given the benefit of the doubt. It may already have been thought generous to interpret Speaker 1's 'halfway to the pegboard' as 'halfway up the pegboard'. Similarly, Speaker 2 defines the location of peg 3 as 'down from your red + opposite your yellow + and opposite the red'. A more mature native speaker of Standard

English would probably prefer to say 'diagonally opposite the yellow', but a test of this type aims to finish up with a measure of descriptive ability uncontaminated by vocabulary differences or spatial skills. Thus a speaker scores the same for saying 'just to the right-hand side' as 'and then along to the right about eight holes'; although the second example is much more precise, the 'just' in the first example is taken as an indication of distance, however vague, and both speakers are credited with having attempted to specify distance and direction.

In the same way that the scoring procedure for the diagram-drawing allocated marks, this method allocates a mark each time the speaker attempts to fill one of the four 'information slots' associated with each peg description, or one of the two slots associated with each elastic band description. This avoids, as far as possible, discriminating against pupils with poor spatial skills – perhaps with right-left difficulties – and pupils who use words like 'diagonally' or 'horizontally' more loosely than more mature speakers who transfer information more skillfully.

Scoring the 'dynamic' tasks

The category of 'dynamic' tasks presents more difficulties; they involve the description of relationships which change over time. In the case of the car crash task, the speaker needs to keep track of the changing positions of the cars in relation to the junction and to each other. In the narrative tasks, the speaker needs to mark temporal and locational shifts in the story as well as giving an ordered account of the various dealings between the individuals in the story. Under this heading of 'dynamic' tasks, we shall first consider narrative tasks.

5.8 Scoring the narrative tasks

In this section we shall look at scoring procedures for two narrative tasks. The first is the cartoon story discussed in the last chapter; it is relatively long, the stimulus materials consist of fourteen separate pictures, and illustrate a story along the lines of boredom-infidelity-boredom. The first three pictures are presented in Appendix A.

Both the input and the output in this task are very rich; the stimulus materials and the descriptions which they generate can only be analysed using sophisticated criteria which it was not necessary to apply to the comparatively simple 'static' tasks. The issue of *reference* is perhaps the most important example of this comparative complexity. Chapter 4 illustrated the need for an adequate narrative to be *referentially explicit*, and gave examples of performances which were unsatisfactory precisely because the listener could not work out which character was being referred to at certain points in the story.

Two further requirements of an intelligible story are clearly marked temporal and locational shifts. Again, Chapter 4 gave examples of adequate and inadequate marking of such shifts.

A fourth and final criterion to be considered here is the inclusion in the story of an adequate amount of information.

There are at least four important dimensions, then, along which narrative performances may be assessed. The second assessment study described earlier in this chapter demonstrated that it is possible to assess performances of simple narrative tasks consistently, in terms of information content and the marking of location, simply by listening to the taped performances no more than twice. Appendix B shows the scoring protocol which the teachers of English were given. As can be seen, the information content which is scored is basic to the telling of the story – a simple description of the characters involved and their activities. A very elaborate telling of the story, with a detailed description of the contents of the room, would almost certainly be to the pupil's benefit if the performance was being scored 'impressionistically'; the scoring procedure in Appendix B allows only the basic information to count to the pupil's credit. This scoring procedure recognises the fact that a perfectly good story can be told using only simple descriptions. This is a satisfactory procedure if we are interested in the ability to *transfer information* rather than any mixture of engagingness/ability-to-tell-a-story/confidence/ personality involved in impressionistic marking.

The ability to include sufficient information would seem to be the least demanding of the four narrative skills we are considering, in that many of the pupils who were given this task produced narratives which contained a reasonable amount of basic information, but which were inadequate in terms of referential clarity and temporal or locational marking.

The marking of locational and temporal shifts seems to be more difficult. The scoring protocol in Appendix B gives one mark if the pupil mentions the location, 'house' or 'living room'. A simple extension which would allow the entire story to be scored for the marking of locational shifts is shown below:

(1) house/living room
(2) bar/party/dance
(3) house/living room
(4) new flat/new house

(5) bar/another dance

One mark is awarded each time the location is specified. Note that a change of location may be announced in a story without specifically naming the location. A story containing '+ + and I think he comes back + +' is judged to be no less adequate than one containing '+ after that the man went home+' as far as announcing the change of location back to the house.

The comment 'then he goes back through into the hall' is sufficient to allow the speaker one mark for a mention of 'house/living room'. It is generally quite clear from the ensuing confusion when a speaker has failed to mark locational shifts clearly, as in example (6) from the last chapter, part of which is repeated below:

(5) he gets dressed and goes to the window and makes himself smart + the lady is still sitting there + with the letter + the man shakes hands + with his friend + and meets a girl + and he starts dancing with her

In this example most listeners would be baffled as to where the dancing was taking place, since the speaker has failed to make it clear.

The marking of such scene changes has much in common with the marking of temporal shifts: the absence of either of them produces the same disorientation in the listener, leaving him with local incidents which do not knit together easily into the overall story. It is also possible to mark both types of shift using similar narrative conventions – one speaker says 'and then we're in a club', using a common scene-changing convention which works equally well for indicating changes in both time and place.

A more complex version of the same events might employ a temporal structure in which the man's boredom and meeting with the younger woman occur in one evening, his wife's overhearing of the telephone call, his explanation and his departure all occur within the following week, followed shortly by the setting up of the new house, with the final ironic sequence perhaps six months later. The meaning of the story does not crucially depend on these complex temporal shifts, however; for the story to be effective, the events simply need to be recounted in the correct chronological order. This can be achieved adequately enough by using a strategy which proved to be common amongst the pupils studied; it consisted of using the historical present tense and casting the story in a *paratactic* structure – a series of simple clauses strung together by *and* and *then*.

(6) + she goes up to her room and falls on the bed and starts crying +

then the man gets his coat on and starts to walk out the door + + the man goes to his girlfriend's house + + and the girlfriend's arm round + the neck

This strategy is not a necessary strategy, of course, simply a common one. It was possible to achieve the same effect by using very few connectives and presenting the story as a string of simple sentences.

(7) there's a man and his wife sitting in the living room + man just gets bored + has a look out the window + decides he wants to go out + gets ready to go to this pub disco + shakes hands with the barman + gets up starts dancing + sits down beside this girl + + back in the house he phones her + his wife comes in the door + his wife sits down

As can be seen, this particular strategy contributes to a rather stilted, formal style, in contrast to those sections of narratives where the speaker uses less common connectives such as *so* and *but*.

(8) the man was bored + so he + walked up and he was looking out the window+

(9) then they are lying on the settee with their arms round each other but the girl seems to be in the huff +

This particular story does not necessarily require speakers to specify time intervals, then, and all of the strategies which we have illustrated were used to produce versions of the story which were adequately marked in terms of temporal structure. Among other sets of pictures used as stimulus materials were two illustrated murder stories, which had a more complicated temporal structure. The stories were temporally complex because they contained references back to the actions of different individuals at the time of the murder. As an example, one of the stories, comprising ten pictures, involved five characters – an old woman, a young woman, a young man, a maid and a police inspector: the murder is discovered by the maid, the young woman and the maid then give their alibis to the police, the police then discover a blood-stained jacket and accuse the young woman and man of committing the murder. The final picture shows the arrest of the young woman.

In order to produce a comprehensible narrative, the speaker had to mark clearly the fact that individuals in the story who were giving their alibis were all referring to the same moment in time in the past. In these stories, failure to mark temporal shifts clearly resulted in stories which were both confused and confusing – often despite evident attempts to include some kind of temporal information. The following performance illustrates inadequate temporal marking.

(10) the maid's gone through to the room + to + give the lady breakfast + she finds her dead she's been stabbed + and the window's smashed and so is the clock + she goes down and phones the police + and + it's + half pase eight + she sees she's to + tells the police that she sees a man going out the window + and then the police come in + + they look at the + the clock that's been smashed + and then + she goes upstairs + and the lady that's been in before + + and it's now ten o'clock and em + + the man and a man and lady were having a drink when the maid sees them + police sergeant takes this down + the maid says + uhm + she's giving the lady that's been killed a cup of tea now + and that was at half past nine + it's now ten o'clock + and the sergeant finds a coat that's all covered in blood + + then she tells + then the sergeant that + it's been a man that's + supposed to have murdered her + and then in the end + it's just this lady that + gets + em + I've forgot the word – oh + that gets arrested

Compare the following two short excerpts from two pupils' narratives, both describing the same illustrated events.

(11) so they go to er + er a sister or somebody + and ask her + and er + but she's standing having a drink with this other guy

(12) and er + then the police was asking the maid + questions about + what she had done + and she had said that she had been through to take tea through to the lady she looks after + and + her and + the man + her daughter and the man + were sitting + having a drink

The events they are describing are contained in a picture which shows the police questioning a maid; the maid is stating (by means of a picture in a 'word balloon') that she saw one of the female characters in the story having a drink with a man. If we ignore the fact that there is more detail in excerpt (12) and the fact that the speaker in extract (11) is inexplicit about the female character(s) involved, it is clear that extract (11) is crucially misleading; the activity of 'having a drink' appears to be taking place in the present, at the same time that the police are taking statements. The speaker in (12) marks the temporal shift involved by using a different tense, saying 'the police *was asking*' and 'she *had been* through . . . and . . . her daughter and the man + *were sitting*'; it is clear from this account that the 'having a drink' occurred previous to the police questions.

A scoring protocol for assessing temporal marking in a narrative would consist of a list of points in the story at which a temporal shift must be clearly marked *for an adequate understanding* of the story; in the example we have looked at it is not necessary for the speaker to do anything else other than to make it clear that the 'having a drink' occurred *before* the police questioning. If the second excerpt was a piece of written English, then it might be considered proper to correct '. . . what she had done + and *she had said* that . . .' to '. . . what she had done + and *she said* that . . .', as the perseveration of the 'had' is not standard written usage. When it is a spoken narrative being assessed for marking of temporal shifts, it is only necessary to draw the pupil's attention to errors of the type shown in the first excerpt, which are grossly misleading to a listener.

A scoring protocol for this particular story would allocate one mark to be awarded if the speaker marked the shift adequately, as in the second excerpt. Changes in time are perhaps most commonly marked by changes in tense, as in the sentence 'and she told them that somebody had come in + and stabbed + the lady she looks after'; in this case, an essential element of the story is the maid's report to the police – that someone had broken in and committed a murder – so the successfully marked temporal shift is awarded a mark. In order to construct a scoring protocol it is necessary to analyse the story and list the information which is essential to an adequate retelling of the story; where there is a temporal shift between an adjacent pair of these events, one mark is allocated for the successful marking of that shift.

As well as using changes in tense to effect the shifts, other devices exist, as shown in the following examples.

(13) + and that was at half past nine + it's now ten o'clock

(14) a man and lady were having a drink when the maid sees them +

(15) + the maid was telling them + er + another lady was telling her a story the night before +

In these examples there is an overt reference to the time of an event or to the fact that another event was going on at the same time; although one type of temporal marking might be thought to be more explicit, or more elegant or to convey additional information, the same score is awarded to any adequate expression of marking.

Temporal marking in narratives is not restricted to giving information about the simple ordering of events; the story used in the first assessment exercise described at the beginning of this chapter is an example of a story which requires the speaker to mention the crucial piece of information that one event was going on *at the same time* as another event. In that particular story, speakers needed to make it clear that a thief was stealing a camera from a parked car, at the same time as a street entertainer, who owned the camera, was escaping from a straitjacket. Appendix B contains a scoring protocol which was used to assess this narrative task; item 3 on the protocol shows that speakers were awarded one mark for clearly marking the fact that the two actions, stealing and escaping, were simultaneous.

In several of the narrative tasks, the listener of the pair was provided with copies of three of the pictures in the cartoon story which the speaker was retelling; the listener's instructions were to listen carefully to the speaker and arrange the three pictures in the order in which it was thought they occurred in the speaker's full version of the story.

It was not our intention to make this listener's task particularly difficult or revealing, nevertheless it represents an alternative way of assessing temporal marking; if the speaker fails to convey the temporal structure of the story, then the ordering of the listener's pictures is more likely to be on the basis of guesswork or the order in which simple information appears in the story. This assessment procedure probably offers less than the straightforward ticking off of explicit temporal marking on a checklist; but it does suggest itself as a useful classroom activity.

So far we have looked at a variety of ways of scoring performances on narrative tasks. We have considered the assessment of information content, the marking of locational shifts and the marking of temporal shifts. The final consideration is the issue of referential explicitness, the ease with which the events in the narrative can be associated with the individuals/entities in the narrative. This is the only aspect of narrative assessment which we would suggest merits transcribing the crucial parts of the narrative; we will not be saying that transcription of all performances is absolutely necessary – simply that judgments concerning the ambiguity of certain nouns and pronouns for instance, are easier to make by referring to a transcription than by referring to a tape recording. Explaining inadequacies in referential explicitness is certainly more difficult than explaining to pupils inadequacies in locational marking, hence there might be pedagogical advantages in transcribing several examples for discussion in class.

Appendix B shows the scoring protocol which was used in the first assessment study, described at the beginning of this chapter. It is a procedure which does not call for the performances to be transcribed; the judge simply listens to each performance no more than a couple of times and fills in the score sheet at the same time. Of the various procedures tested for assessing referential explicitness in narratives, this was the least expensive in terms of time and effort. The essence of this scoring procedure is contained in that part of the instructions which says 'The account of the sequence of events is a success if you are *sure* throughout about *WHO* was involved in each event and *WHAT* the events were.'

The ten possible marks which it is possible to acquire, reflect the essential elements of the story; six of those marks were for referential explicitness, that is, there were six instances in any adequate version where a specified individual must be mentioned. These are repeated below. (The numbers are the same numbers given to the items in Appendix B; the intervening items concern temporal marking and mentions of the actions of the individuals.)

(1) Introduction of *Character A* (the street entertainer escaping from the straitjacket).

(2) Introduction of *Character B* (the thief breaking into cars).

(4) Distinctly mentioning WHO (*Character B*) steals the camera.

(6) Distinctly mentioning WHO (*Character A*) escapes from the straitjacket).

(8) Distinctly mentioning WHO (*Character B*) takes a photograph.

(10) Distinctly mentioning of WHOM (*Character A*) the photograph is taken.

The story could be embellished in many different ways by a competent speaker, but the six references above are crucial to an understanding of *who* did *what*, which is all that this approach requires. The word 'distinctly' is mentioned several times in the scoring instructions, so it is best to emphasise straightaway that this is in the sense of 'unambiguously', as opposed to using a clear, distinct voice or giving the full description of the individual each time; the only criterion is that the listener should understand.

The same applies to the descriptions which speakers give to individuals; all that this system of marking requires is that pupils give descriptions of the individuals in the story which adequately allow the listener to distinguish between those individuals. There is sufficient information in the film version of the story which was shown to pupils for them to be able to refer to one of the individuals as 'Max the Great Escaper' (the words appeared on a box of equipment in the film). Nevertheless, pupils gained only one mark when they were required to introduce this individual, whether they said 'Max the Great Escaper', 'the man who was getting tied up', 'this escape + escapologist', 'this + man eh + he was good at escaping chains and all that', and so on. Similarly, the other character could be introduced satisfactorily as 'this eh man' in the following context.

(16)   the film takes place when Marvo the magician eh + escaper was trying to escape from these ropes he was tied up + and everybody's watching him while *this* eh *man* was going round the cars trying the doors

'Marvo the magician eh + escaper' is inaccurate, strictly speaking, as his correct name is 'Max', but the description is perfectly satisfactory from the point of view of the skills we are assessing. One mark is given for the introduction of the first character (*Character A* on the score sheet). The speaker is next judged on his introduction of Character B. Although the description 'this eh man' is a pretty minimal description, it serves perfectly adequately in this context to introduce a second individual; the listener knows that an individual other than 'Max' is being referred to. A different speaker introduced the second character as 'this thief'; this is clearly a richer description, but it still only collects one mark.

With this particular story, pupils were often content to introduce the second character by means of a fairly minimal description; as we shall see, this may lead to trouble towards the end of the story, where speakers need to explain that the thief in the story breaks into Max's own car, steals a camera and uses it to take a photograph of Max concluding his act. The pupil who elaborated his description of Chapter 2 as 'the thief' copes well.

(17)   then he went to the second car and the door was locked + so then he went to another door that must have been that guy's door + the car + and 'cause it had Max the Great Escaper on and he took his camera + and when the guy got out + the guy the thief took a photo of him

This speaker has hitherto used the term 'guy' to refer only to Max, but right at the end of the narrative he wishes to refer to two male individuals, saying that one took a photograph of the other, and realises that 'the guy took a photo of him' is ambiguous, so he substitutes 'the thief' for 'the guy'. Another referentially explicit story finished in the following way.

(18)   + the man takes a photograph of + the great escaper with his camera

It is clear in this case who is taking whose photograph. Things are very much less clear in the following extract, however.

(19) and he was trying to keep in time with the + the man who was getting tied up + + trying to get finished at the same time as the other
man was + broke into two cars + + and he got a camera + and he
took a photo with the man at the end with the camera

Prior to this extract, the speaker had already introduced two distinct
individuals. A description of this kind clearly requires the listener to do a
lot of 'work', in terms of inferring who is being referred to when the
speaker says 'he' and 'the man'; it is more difficult to keep track of what is
going on in this kind of description than in the previously quoted more
explicit descriptions. When the speaker uses a relative clause, saying 'the
man who was getting tied up', things are clear and this speaker successfully expresses the information that the events were happening simultaneously; from that point on, though, only very minimal descriptions
are used and it becomes successively more difficult to understand who is
doing what in the story. The last two sentences contain references to 'he',
'he' and 'the man' that are ambiguous, in that it is possible to think of
these sentences as describing a story in which either the thief photographed the escapologist or, equally plausibly, the escapologist photographed the thief. Note that, depending on precisely how fragmented the
performance was, it might be possible to feel fairly sure that 'and he got a
camera' meant that the thief stole a camera from one of the cars, but it is
certainly unclear from the final sentence that it was the escapologist who
was being photographed.

This particular narrative task is, in referential terms, one of the
simplest which we have used; it contained only two potentially confusable individuals. The principles adopted in scoring this simplest narrative
nonetheless apply to more complicated types of narrative.

The narrative (part of which is presented in Appendix A, Figures 3a,
b, c) concerning boredom and infidelity, is similar to the previous story
in that there are two characters who may both be referred to as 'she' or
'the woman', and so be potentially confusing to the listener. This story is
referentially more complex, however, in that there are more characters in
all, the female characters disappear and reappear in the course of the narrative, and the relationships between the characters change.

Although the narratives differ in these respects, the same principles of
assessment may be extended to the second narrative. Firstly, it should be
emphasised that a protocol for assessing referential explicitness is only
concerned with those parts in the speaker's version of the narrative which
involve the introduction or reintroduction of a character; these are points
at which a listener needs to be absolutely certain about what is happening

in the story, otherwise things may go radically wrong with the listener's understanding of the story. Much of the detail of the characters' activities in the story will be contained in the protocol which assesses information content, which we have already discussed. This present referential explicitness protocol, given below, is only concerned with the activities of the characters insofar as these activities are the points at which the characters are introduced or reintroduced. Consider the following:

(1) Introduce *Character A* (a male character 'sitting down talking', 'sitting smoking a cigarette', 'sitting in a room')

(2) Introduce *Character B* (a female character 'sitting in the + in the living room', 'sitting in a chair')

(3) Introduce *Character C* (a second female character: 'he just happened to meet this really nice young lady', 'and meets a girl')

(4) Reintroduce *Character B* (she 'starts crying', 'was at the door listening in', 'just happened to be at the door listening')

(5) Reintroduce *Character C* ('and he meets his eh + new girlfriend', 'moving into a house with the girl')

(6) Reintroduce *Character B* ('he meets his wife and she is dancing too', 'she saw his old wife sitting there having a great time with all the men')

A performance judged to be adequate in terms of referential explicitness would be awarded six marks. Clearly it should be possible to arrive at a score after listening to a recorded performance no more than twice. Note that this assesment has nothing to do with the accuracy or appropriateness of the descriptions themselves. Pupils who retold this story referred to Character A, the male character, in a variety of ways, 'Mr Jones', 'the man', 'the guy', and so on; these descriptions are all awarded one mark, corresponding to item (1) in the protocol. Equally, the pupil who says 'There's this couple sitting in the + in the living room . . .' has been explicit enough to introduce Characters A and B, since in Standard English usage 'a couple' standardly implies a man and a woman and is awarded two marks. In order for a speaker to introduce Character C successfully, it is necessary to use a description which makes it clear to a listener that a new character is being introduced. One speaker only used a third person pronoun at this point, 'they started dancing + after that they started talking + + after that they went home'; from this it is not clear that a new individual has been introduced into the story and the listener can only infer that the man in the story is dancing with his wife or with the barman. This speaker clearly fails to gain a mark for item (3).

Item (4) concerns the reintroduction of Character B. Speakers differed according to how many of the events they described at this point in the story, concerning this character. All that is necessary for the narrative to be adequate, for our purposes, is that Character B is successfully reintroduced at this stage in the story. It is not important whether a speaker says that Character B 'is at the door listening in' or simply says that Character B 'starts crying'; one mark is awarded for making it clear that the female character being referred to is not still Character C, who appeared in the previous part of the story. The reintroduction of Character C is scored in a similar way. The objective of this system of scoring, and similar ones, is that it should provide the teacher with a simple quantitative assessment of the pupil's performance in relation to very strictly defined aspects of the task. Insofar as the task has been designed to isolate the use of particular communicative skills, this measure allows the teacher to infer that the pupil is encountering difficulties in deploying that particular skill. The teacher is able to use this diagnosis in order to judge how to proceed with an individual pupil: perhaps the pupil is ready for more advanced levels or types of task, perhaps more time should be spent with the current task, or perhaps the pupil might benefit by briefly returning to the previous level of difficulty in order to learn more about the skill involved. This diagnostic use of the assessment corresponds to 'formative evaluation', as opposed to the 'summative evaluation' involved in awarding a pupil an end-of-school certificate, or in selecting a pupil for a further course.

Note that the general tenor of this kind of assessment makes appeal to what has been termed 'criterion-referenced assessment' – an assessment which is not interested in judging a pupil's abilities in relation to his peers, but rather seeks to say thing about the skills and abilities of a pupil on the basis of performances on tasks which have been specifically designed to test those particular skills and abilities. (For a discussion of criterion-referenced assessment, see S. Brown, 1980.)

To return, then, to the narrative task whose scoring we were discussing, for the particular population of pupils who were given this task, an adequate performance generally consisted of making sufficiently clear references in the case of items (1) and (5), and possibly also being awarded a mark for item (6), the reintroduction of Character B right at the end of the story. Compared with items (1) to (5), item (6) proved to be more difficult for the pupils we tested; relatively few successfully reintroduced Character B at this point in the story. This allows us to make two brief general points, one about assessment, the other about test construction. Firstly, suppose that a pupil's performance deteriorates towards the end of a narrative task; suppose that the pupil fails to transfer some of the information in the final one or two pictures of the narrative, as in (20):

(20) and she looks depressed + and she gets up to the window + the man + looks up + she goes out + with the man + goes to the same club again and starts dancing

In cases such as this, where the pupil clearly fails to score a mark for item (6) as Character B is not reintroduced, it would be inappropriate to use such a performance to say that the pupil is deficient in referential explicitness, according to one system of scoring, *and* deficient in simple description of detail, according to a second system of marking, and so on. In other words, a pupil should not be penalised more than once for one deficient performance or part of a performance.

The second point, about test construction, echoes a point that was made earlier with respect to the diagram-drawing task; in judging performances of that task, it was noted that many things were taken for granted, and did not enter into the information transfer. Lines were always assumed, by default, to be of normal pencil thickness, and so on. There is no merit in including such things in an assessment. Likewise, it may be that certain aspects of a task prove to be outside the normal ability range of the population being tested, in which case it is equally pointless in scoring every performance with respect to that aspect of the task. In the case of the narrative we are currently considering, had the narrative been any longer or any more complex, it might have proved impossible for any pupil to collect a mark for item (6), in which case the scoring procedure or the stimulus materials would be in need of amendment. In reality, the very competent performances succeeded in adequately reintroducing Character B at the end of the story, thus indicating that it was a reasonable goal to set for the rest of the population.

Note that scoring narratives in this way allows us to award almost full marks for referential explicitness (and for other things too) to versions of the story which omit the final reappearance of the man's wife and which therefore fail to convey what would be, for more mature speakers/readers, the irony – the point – of the original cartoon.

A small proportion of narrative performances showed that some speakers were placing an atypical construction on the events in the narrative, as in the following excerpt:

(21) they were sitting on the sofa and they must have been arguing be-

cause then the girl went to the window and started blowing kisses to a man outside + she walked out and the other man behind her unhappy then he went to a dance with his wife before that and the girl went away with another man

Performances such as this are potentially worrying as it is not clear how the end of this particular performance should be assessed. The pupil seems either to have misinterpreted this part of the story or else to have given a version of events which does not square with his own understanding. An important general observation is that the narrative material used in such a task should be pitched at what is a reasonable level of difficulty; this particular story led only a small number of pupils into this kind of comprehension difficulty. More will be said about this later when we consider what is involved in developing new assessment materials, but for the moment it is important to note that there will always exist idiosyncratic performances which it is simply not possible to assess.

When this kind of comprehension difficulty appears to underlie a performance, then that particular performance cannot be used – in its entirety – as a basis for assessment. It is the skill at transferring information which we wish to assess, not skill at interpreting cartoon narratives. In the case of the speaker quoted above, the narrative up to that point was not confused and could be scored in a straightforward way, so it would be possible to produce an assessment from this particular performance simply by assessing the first part. Where comprehension difficulties appear earlier on in a narrative, and cause proportionately more damage to the coherence of the speaker's version of the story, the teacher must be prepared to accept that an assessment cannot be made on the basis of that particular performance. It may be that a discussion with the pupil could make things sufficiently clear for a second attempt to be made, or it may be that the materials themselves could be changed so as to make them more accessible to a particular set of pupils. For assessment which is being used for diagnostic purposes, such performances are only a temporary inconvenience for the teacher wishing to assess a particular pupil's progress; for summative assessment, such performances are more of a problem.

It must be stressed that the point of the exercise is to assess and to develop referential skills. The pupil's understanding of the story is not an end in itself.

Scoring protocols may be developed for any particular narrative simply by listing those points in the narrative at which characters are introduced for the first time and those points at which an individual is reintroduced, where that character is potentially confusable with a previous one as a result of their being the same gender or having other properties in common.

5.9 Scoring the car crash tasks

The descriptive accounts of car crashes, based on a series of pictures, were the second principal type of 'dynamic' task developed. Such descriptions belong to a genre which is very different from that of the narrative tasks we have just considered. There are very clear conventions concerning what an eye witness description should be like, when delivered to the police, for instance, or to an insurance company; there are clear conventions about what type of detail should be included, and how much of it. In many narrative tasks the conventions which decree what is relevant and what is irrelevant, are often far less clear. The descriptive accounts given by the pupils appear to reflect this, together with the fact that the stimulus materials for the car crash task contained far less of what might be called 'peripheral detail', than did the stimulus materials which belonged to other narrative genres. Nevertheless, we still categorise the car crash task as a 'dynamic' task, because, like the narrative tasks, it requires the pupils to generate a temporal structure in which to describe the events, and it requires the individuals taking part in the events to be introduced and reintroduced in such a way that the listener does not confuse them.

It will be remembered that a simple procedure for assessing car crash descriptions was described at the beginning of this chapter in the second assessment study; judges chose one of three possible configurations or ticked a 'Don't know' box according to their interpretation of the speaker's description. Judgments were made of what the configuration of cars was at the beginning, the middle and the end of the sequence of events. A copy of the protocol is given in Appendix B. The number of correct choices compared with the number of incorrect choices and 'Don't know's', will largely reflect the referential clarity of the description; the accurate description of the junction ('the crossroads', 'the crossing', 'a T-junction') plays an important part, but we shall not be concerned with this in this discussion of considering ways of assessing performances of this task.

An inability to choose the correct configuration corresponding, for instance, to the final stage of the events might be caused by any number of more or less serious referential flaws. Consider the following description:

(22) this car was taking over I was standing at the crossroads and this car
      was taking over + a car coming down from + the middle of the cross-
      roads and this car was turning to the right + they banged together
      + because they were going real fast and they couldn't stop + eh
      three of them eh banged into each other + and + banged into the
      one that was going away + pulling out eh just one of them got away
      + from it + + it was quite a bad crash

One of the most confusing things for a listener is that it is not completely
clear from this performance exactly how many cars are involved. Until
the phrase 'three of them', it is possible to interpret the description as referring to either two or three cars; once the listener decides that three cars
must be involved, the speaker says 'and + banged into the one that was
going away', raising the possibility that a fourth car is involved. Compare
this with this next performance from a different pupil:

(23) there's two cars coming down in one line and another one coming in
      the other + and then + the car just came down and the two cars kept
      going and it didn't stop and it went right into another car + and it
      crashed + + + and the other there was another car and it just drove
      away + it didn't stop

This pupil successfully introduces the three cars involved in this incident: we might wish for a more detailed picture, but the speaker has
reached a level of referential success not reached by the previous speaker
in extract (22), in that he has conveyed the information that two cars are
converging on a third car. The rest of the performance is not clear.

There are many advantages if we can extend to this particular type of
'dynamic' task the same principles of assessment of referential explicitness which were used with the narrative tasks. In the narrative tasks,
marks were awarded at points in the performance at which the speaker
successfully introduced one of the characters. In the car crash task the
stimulus materials may be manipulated so as to make introducing the individual vehicles more or less difficult; if speakers are able to introduce
the individual vehicles by such terms as 'a black car', 'a sports car' or 'a
van', then such introductions would seem to be more straightforward
than introductions like 'a car's going along the road' or 'there's two cars
coming one way'. It is easier for a speaker to keep track of simple noun
phrases he has used (such as 'a van'), compared with noun phrases which
have been modified, often by rather lengthy phrases (such as 'going along
the road').

One means of assessing performances is to judge whether or not the speaker has adequately introduced all of the vehicles involved. The last performance which we considered, 'there's two cars coming down in one line and another one coming in the other . . .', was a description of a three-car crash; the pupil has conveyed enough for the listener to determine the number of cars involved, and thus is awarded three points for the performance.

The first speaker we studied, 'this car was taking over . . .', achieved less; two distinct cars are identified by the sentence 'this car was taking over + a car coming down from + the middle of the crossroads', but thereafter although the listener knows that three cars are involved the third car is not adequately distinguished from the first two cars. 'this car was turning to the right' and 'the one that was going away' could easily refer to one of the first two cars. This pupil is awarded two marks for this performance.

One pupil referred to 'two cars + a red car + and a blue one'. Given that the stimulus materials were not coloured, this is clearly a purely personal way of marking the two cars and would not benefit a listener who was shown the photographs at that point. (Other features of extract (24) show considerable imagination; other pupils referred to the drivers of the cars, although none were visible.) The usefulness of this strategy, however, is that it allows the speaker to refer to them extremely successfully in the rest of his description, as can be seen:

(24)   well I was standing at the corner of the crossroads there was + two
       cars + a red car + and a blue one + the red one was going very fast
       + and then the other car was going quite slow as it came to the cross-
       roads + the red one the blue one pulled out from the crossroads
       while the red one tried to take the corner + right fast they suddenly
       + crashed into each other and there was a terrible thud one burst
       into flames

This speaker is given two marks for referential explicitness here, as both of the cars in the crash were distinctly introduced.

Giving a pupil's performance one mark for each entity which is distinctly introduced, is a means of scoring which may easily be accomplished by listening to the recorded performance no more than twice. An assessment of referential explicitness should also concern itself with subsequent references to the car.

In the assessment of the narratives, marks were awarded for the successful reintroduction of a particular character into the train of events. The descriptions we are currently assessing require the pupil to refer to each vehicle at each stage in the events and the sequence of events cannot

be easily divided into discrete stages. In short, there is a danger of referential confusion throughout this type of description, not simply at predictable set points as in the narratives.

Note that a speaker may make it clear to the listener which car he is referring to, in a variety of ways. If a speaker says 'there's one car coming
from the right' and a little later wishes to refer again to that car, then 'the
car that came from the right' is the most elaborate, 'guaranteed' expression to use. There are contexts in which this would be inappropriate,
however, and would be unsuccessful; consider the following extract.

(25) the second car + hasn't got time to avoid + the person who tried +
      who + swerved away to avoid the car that was pulling out + and he
      hits it

In this case a listener might well judge that it was unclear which entity
was being referred to by the expression 'the person who . . . + swerved
away to avoid the car that was pulling out', even though that description
was probably the fullest which would be given; the listener is being given
too much work to do.

Similar problems can occur in the interpretation of pronouns. In some
contexts the meaning is clear, in others it is not. In the following excerpt,
the pronoun 'it' is ambiguous:

(26) the + sort of + reddishy car + is going to turn left + and the other
      car's going to + turn right + + and the sports car + is going right on
      and + the red car's crashed into the back of *it*

In the next excerpt, the listener is in no doubt as to which car 'should stop
and give way':

(27) there's + em a car approaching from the right-hand side + coming
      up to the junction where *it* should stop and give way

In extracts (28), (29) and (30), the speakers fail to give unambiguous descriptions; even though the speakers employ expressions like 'the other
car', which are more elaborate than simple pronouns. In contrast, (31) is
an example of a speaker giving a referentially unambiguous account.

(28) the other car tries to avoid + hitting the car + coming down + and
      the car going smashes into the side of *the car*

(29) that capri + he was coming along and + there was a car taking over
      + another car + + and eh + *car* didn't see it taking over and eh

(30) there's two cars coming down in one line and another one coming in

the other + and then + the car just came down and the two cars kept going and it didn't stop and it went right into *another car* and it crashed

(31) someone was coming down the straight road + and someone was co-coming along + the right road + the right-hand road + and then + the one that was at the right-hand road + was supposed to have wait + waited + at that line + for *the other ones* to come straight down

In extract (32) the speaker devotes more than three-quarters of the words used to expressions which he believes will identify certain cars for the listener – with mixed results:

(32) *the car what came straight* along + and *the other two what came straight to the corner* + hit + *the one what came straight along* hit into *the* + *first car* and *the* + *second one that hit* + crashed into *the other car*

These examples demonstrate clearly that any form of expression may be used to refer successfully, depending on the context. There are contexts in which minimally explicit expressions, such as pronouns, are more appropriate than the more elaborate expressions, just as there are contexts in which only these more elaborate expressions will suffice. It is not possible to teach 'good expressions' which will always be appropriate and which will be guaranteed to succeed.

5.10 Scoring the 'abstract' tasks

Chapter 4 contains a description of the opinion-expressing task which was developed in order to obtain 'pupil-initiated' talk consisting of expressing and justifying an opinion; the aim was to obtain performances which could be assessed against a common set of criteria.

The second assessment study at the beginning of this chapter demonstrated that it was possible for 30 principal teachers of English to judge performances of an opinion-expressing task and to reach a substantial consensus as to how the performances might be graded. Appendix B gives the scoring protocol which was used and which we suggest is suitable for use in assessing pupils' performances in any comparable task in which pupils are asked a question such as 'What do you think about that?', which directs them to deliver an opinion on some topic.

When this task was given to a group of 38 pupils, it was decided to assess each pupil on the basis of his or her reply to the initial question 'What do you think about that?'. Clearly if a pupil is reticent, or gives an impoverished reply such as 'I don't think about it', it is possible to coax responses by means of a series of helpful questions such as 'Do you think he was right?', 'Did you like what he said?', 'Why do you think that?' and so on. Indeed, when the pupils were given this task, they were asked just such a structured series of questions. Looking at their responses as a whole, though, it appeared to be the case that it did not seriously misrepresent their performances if we simply considered their replies to the first question of the series; the first reply was generally typical of the whole performance.

It was possible to categorise these replies using the grades A, B and C defined on the scoring protocol in Appendix B; the definitions are repeated below.

Grade A: opinion expressed
           plus a reason given
           plus an alternative considered
Grade B: opinion expressed
           plus a reason given
           but *no* alternative considered
Grade C: opinion expressed
           but *no* reason given
           and *no* alternative considered

When this task was given to 38 pupils, only two failed to produce a reply in response to the first question; all of the rest could be categorised as Grade A, B or C. If a substantial proportion of replies cannot be graded as A, B or C, then it must be taken to mean that the subject material is inappropriate for such a task or that the questions should be revised.

Apart from a null response, the next least adequate response was one which involved a simple description of the stimulus material with no opinion being given.

(33) well + it's telling you about the belt
(34) it's a man sitting behind a desk talking

Responses such as these are usually relevant and accurate but they must be seen as inadequate, given that the majority of pupils interpreted the question as requiring them to express an opinion. In our assessment, these responses were not distinguished from the following type of response.

(35) he's quite right
(36) true
(37) I don't think about it

(38) I don't think it's true
(39) the belt + don't like it much
(40) I don't agree with it

These brief responses contain opinions and nothing else; they are the minimum adequate response to the question. They are grouped along with the purely descriptive responses into Grade C.

The next most elaborate class of responses contained opinions which were supported by some attempt at a reason or justification. These Grade B responses were usually of the form '(*opinion*), *because* . . .' or '(*opinion*), *if* . . . *then* . . .', as the following examples show:

(41) I think it's wrong *cause* I think the teacher should be able to control the pupils
(42) I disagree with him *cause* there should be other means of punishing people
(43) I think it's quite true *cause* when people are mucking about + once they've been belted
(44) the man was quite right; *if* you do something bad, you're better getting punished like that
(45) well he's right: *if* the teachers didn't have a belt + *then* all their pupils would carry on

Both of these ways of justifying an opinion were classed as Grade B responses. A pupil's response does not have to comply with one of these two ways of linking an opinion and a justification, as the following example shows:

(46) well I think he's getting a bit dramatic at the end by saying education couldn't take place without the belt + but I think it is needed in schools to keep discipline

This example is judged to belong to Grade B. Although no such examples were recorded, it is possible to imagine a very brief reply such as 'I think he's right because it's true'; although this response has the form of a justification, it is contentless and circular and would seem to be more appropriately placed in Grade C. Note that it is not relevant for this assessment that a pupil's justifications may be taken directly from the stimulus material.

Grade A performances, in our assessment, were ones which were judged to contain some considerations of an opposing counter-view to the opinion and justification which had already been expressed. Consider the following response which was judged to be one of the most satisfactory replies to the question:

(47) they should have it cause	Opinion
people don't pay attention	Justification
and it as the only way you can get	
them to pay attention	
and if they put them on detention	Alternative
well some of them don't go	
so it's just as well as having the belt	Conclusion

This pupil gives an opinion, justifies it and then considers an argument against the opinion (i.e. that detention could be used instead), finishing with a conclusion which restates the original opinion. The consideration of an argument against the opinion is the elaboration which distinguishes Grade A performances from Grade B performances. It is reminiscent of the statement in the Bullock Report (*A Language for Life*, HMSO, 1975 para 10.11) that:

The child should be encouraged . . . to develop the habit of trying out alternative explanations instead of being satisfied with one.

The restatement of the original opinion, by way of a conclusion, makes the whole reply more rounded but it adds only to the form of the reply and not to its content. Although the presence of a concluding remark is not critical for the assessment procedure which we have outlined, it may be felt that it should be included in any model reply which pupils might then be encouraged to emulate. Such a model might resemble the following:

  (i) Give opinion;
 (ii) Give reason(s) for;
(iii) Assess arguments against;
(iv) Conclude.

5.11 Testing only what has been practised

The tasks which have been described under the headings of 'static' and 'dynamic' task types all have an intended flexibility, in that any one task type can be used repeatedly with the same pupils, given that the content of the task is different each time. For instance, all that needs to be done with the car crash task is to change the configuration of cars, the type of junction or the types of vehicles involved, and the task can be used several times with the same pupils.

    This means that a particular task type may be used in a series of lessons – in developing referential clarity, for instance – with pupils being given the opportunity to practise with different versions of the task. This is ideally suited to a general procedure of *diagnostic assessment*.

In the work reported in this book, it was almost always the case that the pupil's only previous experience with a particular task was in that specific experiment. For instance, the pupil might have been required to attempt two or more versions of the car crash task in the same experiment, or to participate as a listener while another pupil took the role of speaker. (The effects of this previous experience are described in detail in the next chapter.) In other words, the assessments which are reported in this book were made when the pupil was approaching a particular task 'cold'; the situation was novel. This is very different from the formative evaluation, as envisaged in the school, in which pupils will be assessed according to their performance on tasks with which they are quite familiar as a result of past work; they will simply be encountering a new version of a familiar task type.

Developing an assessment of summarising skills and co-operative tasks
Chapter 4 gave details of two tasks which were not developed as part of the 'static – dynamic – abstract' grid of tasks, but which are clearly tasks which require pupils to deploy sophisticated communication skills. Because one of the tasks is a co-operative task and is conducted with pairs of pupils, it is not appropriate to think of assessing pupils in the same way that individual pupils were assessed using the earlier tasks. Nevertheless, it is possible to approach the other task, the summarising task, in a way that allows a mark to be given to the pupil at the end of the task.

5.12 The summarising task

In the summarising task pupils were required to give spoken summaries or gists of narratives they had previously encountered in a narrative task. (We use the terms 'summary' and 'gist' interchangeably.) Although we have analysed the gists produced, this has been for purposes of comparison with existing theories and descriptions of summarising skills; we have not developed scoring protocols for any of the narrative material used, which could be employed in the classroom to assess progress in developing summarising skills.

The gists which we have so far recorded are principally deficient in terms of length and detail. They are often far too long, despite specific instructions to produce a 'three-line' summary, and they often contain inconsequential detail. We suggest that an assessment of summarising skills should begin with these aspects of the task. The ability to tailor a summary to the required length is the most basic skill in summarising; only when a pupil's summary is recognisably shorter than his full length version of the same narrative will there be any pressure for the various strategies involved in summarising to emerge. The assessment of whether or not a pupil's attempt at a spoken summary is sufficiently short is simply a matter of counting words; the 'three lines' in the instructions should amount to 30 or 40 words.

In order to judge whether or not a pupil has been successful in excluding inconsequential detail from a summary, one needs to have a reliable notion of the relative importance of the various details of the story. We presented the stimulus materials for the narrative task described in Section 4.1.2 to a large number of undergraduates with considerable practice in summarising written material, and obtained three-line written summaries from them. Their responses provided us with a consensus about what were the important points in the story (descriptions of individuals and events). The results of this study largely confirmed our own intuitions about what information should be included by a speaker in an adequate summary. This suggests that in schools it would be sufficient for the teacher, preferably in collaboration with colleagues, to decide which points of a story merited inclusion in an adequate summary. Comparing a pupil's gist with such a list of important information allows a decision to be made as to how successful the pupil has been in excluding inconsequential detail from the gist.

The performances which we have looked at so far suggest that pupils find less difficulty in selecting the more important information than in rejecting the peripheral information. In the 30–40 word summaries which we requested pupils to give, it is a straightforward procedure to separate those parts of the summary which represent important information and those parts which represent trivial information. Initially, no account need be taken of the form in which this information is expressed. The same information may be transferred in a variety of ways, using a variety of linguistic forms; it is important to note that very simple language can be just as effective at transferring information as more complex language. If summarising skills are being analysed from the perspective of transferring information, then an assessment of a pupil's summary may proceed by judging the status of the information contained in the gist.

Depending on the content of the material to be summarised it is possible to penalise the inclusion of trivial information in a gist by, for instance, awarding a penalty mark for each trivial event which is mentioned in the gist, or each trivial character mentioned, or each trivial description which remains attached to a non-trivial character.

As we have said, a variety of strategies appear to contribute towards effective spoken summaries. The nature of the stimulus materials will serve to encourage or discourage specific strategies, so there is an argument for providing pupils with a wide range of materials if summarising skills are being studied.

For instance, a principal strategy discussed by Brown and Day (1983) is that of 'superordination'; this means employing a single, superordinate term in the summary to refer to a number of separate but related entities in the original story. For instance, the original version might include references to trees, plants, fish, land animals and birds, in which case the summary might appropriately refer to 'all living things'. Stimulus materials which present the pupil with several items or individuals, which may be replaced by a single superordinate term, will encourage this strategy. Its assessment will be a simple yes/no judgment according to whether or not the pupil has attempted to operate the strategy.

A third strategy which effective summarising sometimes involves, depending on the stimulus materials used, is for a speaker to begin with a topic sentence or phrase. Appropriate stimulus materials may be given a short title of some kind, to encourage the use of this particular strategy. Often, though, the genre is so clearly marked that this is not necessary as there will already be sufficient encouragement for a pupil to begin a summary by saying 'It's a recipe for . . .' or 'It's a murder story . . .', and so on. Again, the assessment will be a yes/no judgment.

In conclusion, there appear to be many strategies which pupils may employ to produce summaries of material; we have only mentioned three of the commonest. They will be influenced by the form and the content of the material to be summarised. It will often be the case that the same material may be summarised in several different ways, all of them equally adequate but different in that different strategies have been employed. For this reason it would be inappropriate to prescribe a list of 'good strategies' for generating summaries, and to present a model summary for a particular set of stimulus materials. It is the inclusion in the summary of the agreed information, which we are principally concerned with, not the use of particular vocabulary or particular forms of language.

In view of this, it would seem appropriate to ensure that pupils are given as wide a range as possible of material to summarise: it is preferable that the pupil should be acquainted with material before being asked to summarise it. Stimulus materials should be used which are designed to elicit the strategies which we have mentioned. The aim should be to sensitise pupils to the problems of summarising and the range of possible strategies they may select, in order to produce adequate summaries.

5.13 Co-operative tasks: the map task

The map task, described in Chapter 4, represents a means of making pupils aware of some of the very sophisticated skills involved in communicating with a partner who is able, as outside school, to ask questions and comment on what the other is saying to him. Pupils performing in this task may only be assessed as pairs, so it seems to be more appropriate to use the assessment of this task in order to stimulate pupils to consider the skills involved, rather than keeping a record of the assessments as it is possible to do with the previous tasks.

One simple means of assessing co-operation in the transfer of information in the map task, is to inspect the route which one of the partners draws on the unmarked map, from his partner's instructions. The object of the exercise was to replicate the route on the marked map. It will then be possible, when the pupils compare their two maps, for gross differences to be remarked upon. Remember that it is not draughtsmanship which is being assessed, but the ability to recognise that the other person needs to be told whether to go right or left, or up or down at crucial parts of the map. The route which was described may be scored simply by awarding a mark for each feature of the map which the route goes to correctly, given that the route passes that feature on the correct side and in the correct direction.

It will be appreciated that much depends on the precise design of the pairs of maps used. Maps with conflicting features increase the need for sensitive co-operation. The discovery by one partner that the other partner does not share a crucial feature, or that the shared feature is displaced, may be scored in a simple yes/no way; sometimes it is clear from the route produced that a misunderstanding was never resolved, sometimes it is necessary to listen to the taped performance in order to discover the confusion.

It is possible to assess aspects of the taped performance. Listening once to the tape will reveal points in the dialogue at which the pupil who is describing the route is interrupted by his partner, often to request him to slow down, to repeat something, to go back to a certain point on the route, to give extra information, to confirm something which his partner only suspects, and so on. By stopping the tape briefly at these points, it should be possible for the pupils themselves to keep a note of how often a request is ignored, how often it is complied with, and how adequately the information is conveyed.

It will also be possible to recognise specific strategies, especially when pairs of performances are being compared. For instance, one pair of very competent speakers adopted the strategy, when faced with conflicting maps, of listing all of the features which each map possessed, in order to predict where trouble might occur. Pairs of speakers differed also in the length of speaking turn which one partner allowed the other; one partner would sometimes interrupt the other very frequently, simply to acknowledge each instruction with an 'uhuh'. (Pupils might be encouraged to speculate on the advantages of doing this.) Some pupils apparently attempted to reduce the communicative stress of the task by choosing to describe the entire route in one or two turns, brooking no interruption from their partners. Once the performances are listened to, a number of strategies emerge, all with their advantages and disadvantages. Because pairs of speakers differ widely, it will probably be more appropriate to use the task in order to alert the pupils to the strategies we have just enumerated, and to others which emerge, and to the many different aspects of co-operation which this task requires, rather than to construct semi-formal assessments of performance.

To conclude this chapter on assessment, we have considered the three different types of task, categorised as 'static', 'dynamic' and 'abstract', and demonstrated that simple procedures may be applied at all the grades of difficulty of a task in order to arrive at an assessment of a performance which reflects, as objectively as possible, a pupil's information transferring skills. We have laid out the arguments elsewhere in this book for concentrating on these particular skills, nevertheless, we recognise that teachers may well be concerned with other aspects of pupils' speech. The assessment procedures which have been described will contribute towards an assessment profile of an individual pupil; alongside other judgments the teacher may wish to make about the pupil's spoken language skills – such as grammatical correctness, use of appropriate vocabulary, fluency, pronunciation and so on – the assessment of information transfer will exist as a proper part of the overall assessment profile, as in Table 5.3.

Table 5.3 An assessment profile

Date	Type of Speech	Fluency	Pronunciation	*Information Transfer*	Vocabulary	....	....

6 Helpful conditions: overcoming the problem

In Chapter 5, we showed how pupils' performances could be assessed, and in the present chapter we will use these types of assessment of task performances to demonstrate those conditions under which pupils show progress. We believe that one of the advantages of the task-based approach which we adopt, is that the teacher or researcher can manipulate the conditions under which any pupil performs a task, and, with the aid of the objective assessment procedure for that task performance, ascertain which conditions are most conducive to success for particular pupils in particular tasks.

In the rest of this chapter, we will report on the conditions which we have investigated in this way and suggest from these controlled investigations, procedures which might usefully be adopted in the classroom.

6.1 Practice on the tasks

When we were recording pupils performing the various tasks which we devised, as the examples in Chapter 4 illustrate, we found that on almost all our tasks some speakers at least were performing less than adequately. There was much room for improvement in many of the performances, particularly at the more difficult levels, and on the more difficult task types. We tried to identify the reasons for some of the poorer performances we recorded, so that we could provide conditions which would alleviate the problems which these speakers were having with our tasks.

The first obvious explanation which we felt might be useful in this respect was the novelty of the situation in which the speakers were placed. We discussed in Chapter 4 how we felt that the novelty of the task content and the variety of the types of tasks, which we presented to our speakers, were a motivating factor in eliciting both extended amounts of speech and apparently co-operative behaviour from our speakers. However, whilst in general the novelty of the situation may indeed be motivating for speakers, the unfamiliarity of the tasks and their demands, may leave some speakers uncertain of what is required of them in a particular task. As a result of this uncertainty they may produce less than adequate performances, which may not reveal their true abilities. We decided therefore to experiment with performances under a number of different controlled conditions. The first study offered speakers repeated opportunities to perform certain tasks and so to investigate the effect of practice on the performances of a given task.

6.1.1 The effect of practice on performances of 'static' tasks

The first study we conducted investigated the effects of practice on speakers' performances of 'static' tasks. In analysing many hours of recordings of speakers' performances of 'static' tasks such as the diagram-drawing task and the pegboard task (see Appendix A for full descriptions of these tasks) we found that many speakers had not performed very successfully. From the assessment procedures described in Chapter 5, we were able to observe that the speakers often failed to specify fully the information which they were communicating to their hearers. So some speakers would omit necessary information about the sizes or distances involved in their instructions, or they would omit to tell their hearers where, on the page or pegboard, to begin, or they would give full specification for some but not all of their instructions. In general some speakers produced performances which took no account of their hearer's need for fully explicit instructions, or failed to produce consistent instructions. By providing repeated opportunities for a group of speakers to perform these tasks, we hoped to discover if practice would alleviate either or both of these problems and result in better performances.

In our study of the effect of practice, we recorded a group of speakers performing these tasks on two occasions, one week apart and compared their performances on first and second attempts. We found that, on average, speakers produced 60% of the required information as shown on the scoring protocols for diagram and pegboard tasks, on their first attempts and 62% of the required information on their second performances. This small numerical difference when tested statistically was shown to be a chance fluctuation. Similar results were found with a large group of young speakers who were given two opportunities within a single recording session to perform such tasks: again, practice in speaking did not lead to significantly improved performances. A summary of the results and the statistical analyses performed on them is shown in Appendix C. (Full details of these studies are given in Anderson, Yule and Brown, forthcoming.) We concluded from these studies that merely offering speakers practice in speaking on a task did not lead to any significant improvement in performance.

If practice in speaking did not lead to improved performances, what other task conditions could be manipulated to help speakers overcome their difficulties? From informal discussions with the pupils after our recording sessions, it seemed to be the case on many occasions, that the pupil who had taken the hearer's role in the task made more insightful comments about the tasks than the speaker. This observation made us recall research on very young children's communicative skills where it was suggested that experience in the hearer's role might help overcome 'egocentric' performances on tasks: that is, performances where the young speaker does not take the hearer's viewpoint or knowledge into account. (See Dickson, 1980, for a recent review of this research.) We therefore decided to test the effect of prior experience in the hearer's role, on subsequent spoken performances to see whether we would find the same beneficial effects in our teenage population.

6.1.2 The effect of experience in the hearer's role on performances of 'static' tasks

To study the effect of experience in the hearer's role, we first compared the performances of those pupils whom we had recorded in two sessions one week apart. These speakers had initially taken the speaker's role in the first week, and at that same session, had then taken the hearer's role in listening to another pupil giving instructions on a different version of the same task. One week later, we recorded their performances on other versions of two 'static' tasks – the diagram and the pegboard tasks. In their initial spoken performances, the speakers in this study produced, on average, 58% of the required information in their instructions on the two tasks. On their second performances one week later, having taken the hearer's role, the average score rose to 78% of the required information. This is a significant improvement.

A larger second study was conducted in which performances of speakers who had experience in the hearer's role immediately prior to performing these tasks as speakers, were compared with the performances of their partners in the recording session who were not given this opportunity. The pupils who had experience in the hearer's role performed significantly better, and very similarly to the pupils in the corresponding condition of the first study. They produced average scores of 75% of the required information, compared to the pupils who lacked this experience, who produced average scores of 62% of the required information. Table 6.1 shows the plan of these two experiments. Again details of the results and analyses are shown in Appendix C.

Table 6.1 Plan of experiments to test the effect of experience in the hearer's role on performances of 'static' tasks

Experiment 1 (Average scores shown in brackets)

Speakers without experience of hearer's role	Speakers with experience of hearer's role
Week 1 Session 1 Pupils take speaker's role (60%) *Week 1 Session 2*	Pupils take speaker's role (58%) Pupils take hearer's role
Week 2 Pupils take speaker's role (62%)	Pupil's take speaker's role (78%)

Experiment 2

Speakers without experience of hearer's role	Speakers with experience of hearer's role
Week 1 Session 1 Pupils take speaker's role (62%) *Week 1 Session 2* Pupils take hearer's role	Pupils take hearer's role Pupils take speaker's role (75%)

6.1.3 Examples of performances from speakers with and without experience of the hearer's role

In the examples below, we see fairly typical performances of the 'static' tasks by different speakers, two speakers who only spoke on the tasks and two speakers who had prior experience in the hearer's role. (The diagram and pegboard being described by the speakers are shown in Figures 1 and 2 or Appendix A.)

(1) Diagram-drawing task. Speaker without experience of hearer's role.
     three + + in orange a line under it + then a square in black + then
     a line under the square in + orange

(2) Diagram-drawing task. Speaker with experience of hearer's role.
     about a third of the way down from the middle of the page + on the
     right-hand side + there's a large box + about two centimetres +
     each + line + it's a square directly below it about + half cen-
     timetre there's a red line + the full width of the + line of the square
     + going back to the + top of the square + about a centimetre
     above that + there's a red line + about half the size of the box +

and about another centimetre up + there's a + number three + in
black + which is quite large

(3) Pegboard task. Speaker without experience of hearer's role.

there's a yellow + dot and + down from that there's a red one + directly below + no straight below a few spaces away + then + it's
the same on the other side + eh going the other way + instead of
going down go across + then put two green elastic + join all eh the
bits up + oh on the other one there's a blue and a red + down a bit
+ then directly above the red + there's a blue + then join all the
elastic bands up + the red ones + on the first one you done there's
a blue one that goes between your + right bottom one + and your
left top one + which goes right in the centre + of both of them

(4) Pegboard task. Speaker with experience of hearer's role. (All subject
pairs received the same instructions. It is merely accidental that this
hearer participated more than others.)

Speaker: halfway down from the right-hand side + and put in a pink
peg + pink + then + go to your right halfway along the
board + and put in a yellow + then come down + down so
the two + put in another red peg + so the two red so the
two red pegs are opposite each other + making a triangle +
you come down from the yellow peg straight down

Hearer: oh aye I get you now

Speaker: so the two pink pegs + are diagonal opposite each other +
then go along and put in a blue peg at the left-hand side +
to make a square + so it makes a square + then get a green
elastic band + put it round the two pink ones and the yellow + leaving out the blue + now come along from the +
bottom bottom right-hand pink + and go right along to the
right-hand side + so the blue pink and blue and put in a
blue peg

Hearer: blue peg?

Speaker: yes so you've got a blue pink and blue all in line + right go
down go down to the bottom right-hand corner and put in
a pink + straight down

Hearer: from the blue?

Speaker: yes + from your right-hand blue + right at the bottom +
then go halfway along till you come underneath your pink
again + then put one in there to make triangle

Hearer: what colour?

Speaker: blue + straight underneath your pink

Hearer: straight under it?

Speaker: no not under it pink straight along from your right-hand
           pink + then take a pink elastic band and put it round your
           + your blue your blue and your pink

The point we wish to illustrate with these examples is not the details of
the scoring of these tasks, which would result in higher marks being
awarded to speakers (2) and (4), but the more general impression which
these performances give of a real appreciation of the demands of the task
and the speaker's attempts to provide sufficient explicit information to
allow their hearers to complete the tasks successfully.

The speakers in (2) and (4) are not adequately informative in all cases,
of course. For example in (2), the speaker does not mention the colour of
the square which he tells his hearer to draw, and in (4) the speaker incorrectly assumes that by telling her hearer to place a peg 'so the two red
pegs are opposite each other + making a triangle' she has specified a particular location. Although these speakers are not performing the tasks
perfectly they appear to be producing speech which is markedly more
effective in its transfer of information than the kinds of performance
shown in examples (1) and (3).

The kinds of omission of information which are illustrated in (1) and
(3) suggest that these speakers really do not appreciate the requirements
of their hearers in these tasks. If we have access to the diagram or pegboard which these speakers are describing then we can follow what these
speakers mean and indeed realise that as descriptions these performances
are not inappropriate. But as instructions to hearers who have no other
source of information, these performances are inadequate. The instructions given do not take the hearers' lack of knowledge into account, and
so are not explicit or informative enough to allow the hearer to complete
the drawing of an exact copy of the diagram or to arrange the pegs
appropriately. The way in which speakers launch into descriptions of the
elements in the task without telling their hearers how to orientate their
drawing or pegs at the start of the performance seems particularly indica-
tive of this failure to appreciate the hearer's point of view.

The length of the performances also seems to indicate that the speakers
in (2) and (4) are making a greater effort to inform their hearers
adequately. Some of the 'extra' speech results from these speakers providing extra information. In (2), the speaker specifies the distances,
dimensions and positions of the elements in the diagram compared to the
very minimal information provided by the speaker in (1). Interestingly,
some of the extra information is actually repetition of information, for

example at the beginning of (4), where the speaker repeats the colour of the first peg, and in the instruction 'red peg + so the two red so the two red pegs are opposite each other'. Similarly instructions are also on some occasions redefined with extra information added, but this extra information is, strictly speaking, redundant and as such does not contribute to the scores the performances would obtain under our scoring procedures. Our scoring procedures only score minimal requirements, and teachers might wish to encourage such additional efforts informally. For example, in (2) the speaker describes one of the elements involved as a 'box', which we consider from the performances of many speakers and hearers in this population to be synonymous with 'square', yet this speaker both mentions that each line of the box is two centimetres long and then also adds 'it's a square'. Similarly in (4), the speaker says not only which pegs the green elastic band has to surround, but also adds which peg has to be left out. The speaker also instructs the hearer where to place a peg, saying 'now come along from the + bottom bottom right-hand pink + and go right along to the right-hand side' which defines the location and then adds the redundant information about three pegs being in line. Again when instructing the hearer about another peg the speaker says 'from your right-hand blue' (speaker names this peg incorrectly – the peg in question is actually pink) 'right at the bottom + then go halfway along' which, apart from the colour confusion, identifies a particular location, but again the speaker adds the redundant description 'till you come underneath your pink again'. This kind of repetition and redundancy is largely absent from the performances of speakers who have not had experience in the hearer's role, and adds to the general impression that speakers who have had this experience understand their hearer's requirements and are striving to provide helpful and informative instructions in these tasks. The speaker realises from his own experience of trying to complete the task from a partner's less than adequate instructions, that in these tasks the hearer requires fully explicit information and that only the speaker can provide such information. Thus in his own subsequent spoken performances a speaker with this experience really understands what is needed and tries to provide the required information in his instructions.

6.1.4 The effect of task difficulty, task order, and practice in the hearer's role on the performance of 'static' tasks

We have claimed that one of the benefits of the task-based approach to teaching information transferring skills, is that a syllabus can be devised which includes tasks of known and graded levels of difficulty. One of the first task conditions which we wished to investigate systematically was the performance of speakers on tasks which we had devised to represent different levels of difficulty. We were anxious to discover if our assigned levels of difficulty in a given task type would be reflected in the performances of speakers.

We began by investigating the performances of speakers on two levels of difficulty in the static diagram-drawing and pegboard instructions. Each speaker was presented with one task at an 'easy' level and one task at a 'difficult' level (cf. Appendix A). We recorded and scored the performances on the tasks and then compared the scores for the two levels of difficulty. We treated the two tasks as equivalent, firstly because in principle we believed that they were both testing very similar information transferring skills involving the accurate description of objects and their spatial relationships. Secondly, because in an earlier study we had found a statistically significant correlation between scores on the two types of tasks (Pearson's r = .76, p<.01). This means that, in general, a speaker who performs well on the diagram task also performs well on the pegboard task and a speaker who performs badly on one will usually also perform badly on the other. The results we obtained showed that the average score for speakers on the easy version of both tasks was 74% of the required information provided, compared to an average score of 51% on the difficult version of the tasks.

In a second study, we tested another group of speakers on easy and intermediate versions of the same tasks. We found that scores for the easy tasks averaged 74% compared to average scores on the intermediate versions of tasks of 64%. Again, the intermediate tasks used in this study are shown in Appendix A.

From the results of these studies, we concluded that at least for 'static' tasks of the instructional kind, the features of the task stimulus material which we had manipulated to make the task appear more or less difficult, affected speakers' performances in the predicted direction; speakers were indeed more successful on those levels of tasks which we predicted would be easier.

Our next concern was to investigatre the effect on speakers of having the tasks of various degrees of difficulty presented in different orders. We wished to test, in particular, if our notion of a syllabus which consists of graded tasks presented in ascending order of difficulty, would be helpful for use in schools. To test this idea, we compared the performances of two groups of speakers who were presented with two 'static' tasks of easy and intermediate levels of difficulty. One group received the tasks with the easy task first, whilst the other group received the tasks in reverse order. As in our other studies, the diagram and pegboard task which were used in this study were used as comparable alternatives, and so for half the pupils the easy task was the diagram task whilst for the other half, the easy task was the pegboard. The results showed that speakers given an easier task first, perform better on the following intermediate-level task than speakers who are given the intermediate-level task to begin with. That is, presenting tasks in an ascending order of difficulty produces better performances on the more difficult tasks.

We might speculate that there are two possible factors which contribute to this result. One is that pupils find it very easy to understand the requirements of the easy version of a task and having understood the task type, are able to transfer that understanding to the more difficult version. The second is that pupils may gain in confidence from having had the experience of feeling successful in a previous performance.

The results of this series of studies of the effects of task conditions on speakers' performances, confirm our general belief that one of the advantages of our task-based approach to training oral communication skills, is that the task conditions can be systematically manipulated in a manner which is beneficial to the pupil. We have found that a number of simple manipulations have considerable beneficial effects. These conditions, such as providing the speaker with prior experience in the hearer's role in the task, sensitise the speaker to the requirements of the task.

We found that the best spoken performances occurred when speakers both had experience in the hearer's role and also received the tasks in ascending order of difficulty. Under these circumstances, speakers were significantly more successful on the more difficult tasks than in any of the other conditions we investigated. In fact, in these conditions, the general effect of task difficulty was overcome. In terms of the percentages of required information provided in the speaker's instructions, the average score was substantially higher (20% to 33% higher) than in the other conditions. The magnitude of the beneficial effect of this simple combination of task conditions suggests that this finding, derived from a systematic experimental investigation, also has considerable educational significance.

Overall the results of these investigations of 'static instructional tasks' suggest that, by combining experience of the hearer's role with a series of graded tasks of ascending order of difficulty, the teacher would be able to present pupils with optimal conditions which would allow the speakers to complete information transferring tasks successfully. This outcome might well be beyond their oral communication skills in less helpful circumstances.

6.1.5 The effect of practice on performances of 'dynamic narrative' tasks

Having found that manipulating task conditions could have beneficial effects on the performances of speakers on 'static' tasks, we wanted to know if the same kinds of manipulation would have similar effects on the performances of 'dynamic' tasks.

The first study we conducted investigated the effect of simple practice on performances of a narrative. In this study, twenty-five speakers were recorded performing the story-telling task described in Chapter 4, on two occasions one week apart. The stories told by all speakers in the two sessions were transcribed and the stories were analysed for the amount of detail they contained. The details depicted in the cartoon stimulus material for the 'narrative' task were simply set out as a list, which totalled sixty-seven points, and one mark was awarded each time one of these details was mentioned in a speaker's story. (An example of this procedure is shown in Appendix B, where the scoring procedure for the first picture in the stimulus material is shown with examples of the scores for the beginnings of some speakers' stories.)

We found that the average number of details given by speakers was greater in the second session. (Details of the results and analysis are given in Appendix C.)

It appears from the results of this study that we have found a beneficial effect of practice in 'dynamic' tasks which seems at first to be inconsistent with the findings we reported concerning 'static' tasks. Following more careful consideration of the two sets of results, however, we believe that this inconsistency is more apparent than real.

In this study of story-telling with practice, we have found that speakers include, on average, five extra items of information on their second attempt at the task. But when we considered the performances of the speakers in both sessions we found that the majority of the stories were quite adequate in terms of the amount of information they contained. Given that there were fourteen pictures used as stimulus material in this task, the average amount of detail provided by speakers is two and a half items of information per picture, in session one, and three items of information per picture, in session two. Both from listening to the stories, and observing the hearers who were deciding which of a set of pictures belonged to the story they were being told, the majority of speakers could describe the information contained in the pictures quite adequately. Only a very small number of speakers produced stories which seemed to be inadequate in terms of the information they contained, and these speakers tended to produce stories which were similarly impoverished in both recording sessions.

From these detailed analyses of performances, we concluded that practice enabled speakers to improve those aspects of the task which they had largely already mastered. Intuitively, this seems to agree with one's own experience: we all enjoy repeating and improving the skills we already possess. We are all rather less eager merely to have another attempt at some task which makes us feel unsure or unsuccessful. The results of the 'static' task experiments suggest that where speakers have real difficulties in understanding, and in complying with the demands of a particular task, then repeated opportunities to attempt the task in the speaker's role will not help the speaker overcome these difficulties.

The educational implications of these findings seem to be that giving speakers experience in the hearer's role is more helpful than simple practice in tasks where a speaker is having real difficulties in appreciating what a particular task requires. In tasks where speakers are largely successful in meeting a particular task demand, then repeated practice may enable them to improve further their performance in this respect, and may indeed be a pleasant and generally motivating experience.

6.1.6 The effect of practice on the performance of 'dynamic' tasks (the car crash task)

We have investigated the effect of practice on the 'dynamic' tasks in the previous study by examining how much information speakers included in their stories on two separate occasions. Our claim was that this was an aspect of story-telling which the majority of our population of speakers found well within their oral communication abilities and thus simple practice produced beneficial effects. In the next study we investigated the effect of practice, compared to the effect of experience in the hearer's role, on those aspects of 'dynamic' tasks which we have evidence to suggest that speakers find more difficult.

In Chapter 4, we discussed the characteristic requirements of 'dynamic' tasks, and stated that a major aspect was the need for speakers to be referentially explicit in their use of language. That is, speakers have to describe clearly which characters or objects are involved at any particular point in their description or story. We illustrated from several stories produced by speakers that, where this requirement was not met, the resulting story was confusing for the hearer. We suggested that the greater the number of same-gender characters or objects involved in a 'dynamic' task, the greater the difficulty the task would present for the speakers. From recordings we have made of speakers performing 'dynamic' tasks with several such same-gender characters, we discovered that this was a task requirement which presented real difficulties for many speakers. This therefore seemed a promising subject for investigation in a study where the task conditions would be manipulated as in the studies described earlier in this chapter.

We selected the car crash task (see Appendix A for details of this task) for this study because it was a task in which referential explicitness was a crucial requirement. In a description of a car crash, the hearer cannot use general knowlege to discriminate between inadequately specified vehicles. All cars and vehicles do fairly similar things, and if the speaker fails to distinguish clearly which car is being described at any point, the hearer will gain a totally confused or inappropriate impression of the events being described. Our initial recordings of speakers performing this type of task suggested that many speakers failed to appreciate the need for explicit and consistent descriptions of the vehicles involved in their eye witness accounts of the accident, and so many performances were inadequate in terms of referential explicitness.

In the study of the effect of practice and experience in the hearer's role, we presented each of fifty-four pupils with two car crashes to describe to a hearer, in the way described in Appendix A. Thus for each speaker we had two performances to compare. Half the speakers we recorded performed early in the recording session and therefore only had experience in the speaker's role, whilst the other half had been in the hearer's role during these performances before they subsequently performed as speakers, and this group represented the speakers with experience in the hearer's role. Each speaker was presented with stimulus material which in one task contained two cars or vehicles, and in the other task contained three cars or vehicles. Full details of the design of this study are given in Anderson (forthcoming). The study was designed to give information about (a) the effect of simple practice in speaking, (b) the effect of experience in the hearer's role, (c) the effect of combined experience of both, and (d) the effect of the level of difficulty of the task as defined by the number and type of vehicles involved.

All the performances were recorded, transcribed and then scored for referential explicitness. For this study we considered every occasion on which a speaker described a car or vehicle, and as described in Chapter 5, if the description used was identical to the way in which the speaker initially described the car or vehicle in question, and the description was different from the way in which other cars and vehicles were described then the description was considered successful. The number of successful and unsuccessful descriptions in each type of car crash, and for each condition of the study was totalled, and overall percentages of success were calculated. The results of this study are shown in Table 6.2.

Table 6.2 Average percentages of referential success in car crash task

Speakers without experience in hearer's role		Speakers with experience in hearer's role	
1st Performance	2nd Performance	1st Performance	2nd Performance
56%	62%	68%	85%
Overall average 59%		Overall average 77%	

Type of task	
2 cars/vehicles	3 cars/vehicles
81%	54%

Statistical analyses of the results (full details in Appendix C) showed that there was a significant beneficial effect overall in having been given experience in the hearer's role, but no such effect of simple practice in speaking. When the relationship between the two effects of practice and experience in the hearer's role was tested, we found that the real improvement came where the two effects were combined. Only the scores for speakers who had experience in the hearer's role and who were performing their second task were significantly higher than the other scores. As can be seen from the percentages shown in Table 6.2, not only is this a statistically significant result, but the size of the difference involved, an average improvement of nearly 30% over the least helpful 'first task, no-hearer-experience, condition', suggests that this combination of task conditions can be an important beneficial factor in eliciting much more successful performances from speakers.

The average success scores which were found for each of the different task types again confirm that levels of difficulty can be preset according to objective criteria such as the number of objects involved, and that these levels will be reflected in the performances of speakers.

6.1.7 Examples of performances of car crash descriptions

Example (5) is by a speaker who was describing his first car crash and who did not have experience in the hearer's role. The subscripts after each descripiton of a car indicate whether the expression used is scored as (s) successful or (u) unsuccessful.

(5) the car_s went + the car_s came from + the right-hand side and tried to cross + the road + up to + in front of it_u + and it_u turned + and the other car_u tried to turn + the car_u behind it_u crashed + into the right car_u

Example (6) is by a speaker who is describing her second car crash and therefore represents a performance after practice in the speaker's role in the task.

(6) there was two $cars_s$ coming + it's a crossroads + there's two $cars_s$ coming + down the road and there's one car_u going + right across + and the first car_u + stops and lets + one of the $cars_u$ round + and then it_u starts and then the other car_u + comes + right down + without stopping and + the car that let one of them $past_u$ + goes smashes right into it_u

Example (7) is from a speaker who is describing his first car crash but who has had prior experience in the hearer's role.

(7) two + one car_s was overtaking + a car with some black tyres on the $roof_s$ + the other car_s was coming in from the left-hand side a sports car_s + as the car_u was taking over the sports car_s stopped + then moved on moved on + the $mini_u$ + the sort of $mini_u$ + turned to the left + and the + the custom car_u came right across + and hit the sports car_s + and both bonnets were sent + flapping up

Example (8) is taken from a speaker who is describing her second car crash, and so has had practice in speaking and who has also had prior experience in the hearer's role.

(8) coming in from + the + right is a a black a blackish car + with a white top_s+ and coming up from the top is + a $sports_s$ and just another car_s + a lightish sports car_s and another car_s + right + the black car with the white top_s starts + just starts just starts to move out + so the car the black car with the white top_s moves out + and + just turns the way the + other two $cars_s$ are coming + and the sports car_s turns right + the car $behind_u$ the sports car_s just crashes into the sports car_s

All these examples are performances elicited by stimulus photographs containing three cars involved in an accident. Due to the failure of the speakers in (5), (6) and (7) to be sufficiently referentially explicit, the number of cars involved is very hard to determine from these performances. Although each speaker fails on several occasions to be adequately explicit, we should note that they fail using different forms of language.

The speaker in (5), is fairly typical of those speakers who described their first car crash without having been in the hearer's role. The language used to describe the cars involved in the accident is uninformative, the expressions used, for example 'the car', 'it' and 'the other car', fail to distinguish between the three cars involved, and the hearer listening to this description would be unable to follow the events being described.

Example (6) which represents a performance of a speaker who has had practice in speaking in this task, is almost as hard to follow, because of the speaker's failure to cope with the need for clear explicit descriptions.

In this performance there is no evidence that simple practice has encouraged the speaker to use more informative language. The expressions selected to refer to the various cars, 'the first car', 'one of the cars', 'the other car', 'it', are similar in form to the expressions selected by speakers on their first performances, and similarly fail to refer adequately.

As we found when we examined performances of 'static instructional tasks', speakers often seem unable to take their hearer's perspective into account, and they do not appreciate that, with only inexplicit and uninformative language available, the hearers will not be able to understand what is being described. This seems to be a difficult fact for speakers to grasp, and as in our previous studies, simple practice in speaking does not effectively overcome the speakers' failure to appreciate this requirement.

In example (7), the speaker has had prior experience in the hearer's role, and from our previous studies we would expect that this would lead such a speaker to be more aware of the hearer's need for full and informative descriptions. The overall average success rate in this condition, 68%, was not in fact significantly better than the performances in the two previous conditions, and as we can see in example (7), there are many expressions used in this condition which are unsuccessful. If we consider in some detail the language used in (7), again a reasonably representative performance, then we observe that although the overall success rate is similar to the previous conditions, the forms of expressions used by the speaker are rather different.

In (7) the speaker uses the expressions such as 'a car with some black tyres on the roof', 'the mini' and 'the custom car', which are more discriminating and informative for the hearer than the kind of language used in (5) and (6). Even where a less informative expression such as 'the other car' is used, the speaker seems to realise that this uninformative-ness is unhelpful, and redescribes the car in question with the more helpful description 'the sports car'. This speaker is using a variety of types of language, apparently in an attempt to describe precisely and distinguish the cars involved in this accident. The speaker does seem to be aware of the hearer's need for explicit information. However, where this speaker is very much less successful, is in realising that the language used in this task must not only be explicit enough for the hearer to be able to distinguish the cars concerned, but must also be *consistent* enough to allow the hearer to know that the car which was originally introduced as 'overtaking' is the same car later described as 'turning left' or 'pulling out'. The only way the hearer will understand the events is if identical or very similar expressions are used to refer to the same car throughout the description. In fact (7) seems potentially misleading because the speaker has grasped the need to be explicit but failed to be sufficiently consistent in his use of language. The crash being described seems to involve up to six separate cars as each specific description appears to introduce a new car into the events.

In (8) we have a performance from a speaker with experience in the hearer's role as well as practice in speaking, and only this combination seems to result in a description which is largely successful in terms of referential explicitness. The speaker in this example, like the speaker in (7), strives to provide the hearer with informative descriptions, often elaborating initial descriptions. This speaker also demonstrates the ability to use these descriptions consistently.

For this very difficult task, describing a sequence of events involving three similar same-gender participants, the speaker needs to be fully explicit and informative in selecting descriptions for the cars involved, and experience in the hearer's role sensitises speakers to this task requirement. In this complex task the speaker also seems to need practice in speaking on the task to be able to use language consistently enough to communicate successfully the events to the hearer. The combined experience results in performances which are considerably more effective than those produced in the other task conditions and again suggests that these conditions have educational potential in training transactional skills.

6.2 Working in groups to improve performances

Having discovered a series of helpful task conditions which led to improved performances by speakers in a series of large scale experimental studies, we wanted to see if such task conditions could be used profitably in a more informal way which might be of relevance to classroom practice.

As we are researchers, rather than practising teachers, we have conducted our study not as a classroom exercise but in conditions which are as close as possible to those in the school.

We first selected a group of pupils from a school we had previously visited twice, so the pupils had spent about an hour and a half with us before the current study began. These pupils had previously produced performances which we had assessed as being amongst the less successful. We chose them because this seemed a more stringent test of our procedures and because such pupils were obviously most in need of help in learning to transfer information.

We had limited access to these pupils and so instead of a series of forty-minute lessons over a period of weeks, we had to conduct fairly intensive training and testing sessions all within a single day.

The study was conducted as follows. In the morning, a group of five pupils listened initially to taped performances of a selection of tasks. The pupils individually tried to complete the appropriate hearer's task whilst listening to the tape. At the end of each performance the group compared their completed tasks and discussed among themselves and with one of the researchers, the difficulties they had experienced and the differences among their tasks which had resulted from inadequacies in the speaker's performance. As the performances which they listened to were far from perfect, (indeed they were selected to be similar to the kinds of performances these pupils themselves had previously produced) the discussion of what the speaker should have said was usually lively, and showed that the pupils were just as sensitive to the inadequacies of other speakers' performances as the researchers. The taped performance was then repeated and stopped at appropriate points for detailed discussion of what other piece of information or different form of expression would have been more helpful to the hearers. Members of the group were then given an opportunity to perform an alternative version of the task in question, a version which was recorded, while the rest again acted as hearers. Both during and after this performance, the hearers were allowed to comment or ask for clarification.

One of the aims of this study was to discover whether any insights which the speakers gained might be generalisable to other tasks on later occasions. The tasks selected for the morning training session were therefore different in content from the tasks presented in the afternoon testing session. Whereas the main training session used the 'static' peg-board task, in the afternoon session we tested a variety of other 'static' tasks, as well as the pegboard task.

In the testing session a variety of 'static' and 'dynamic' tasks were used and overall the performances we recorded from the pupils were considerably more effective than the performances we had previously recorded from the same speakers. In general we found that our training session had had a beneficial effect on their performances. In particular, the performances showed that the speakers were making an attempt to give full and explicit information to their partners. In the examples which follow, of the performances by three speakers in the group before and after training on three different tasks, there is evidence for this kind of increased appreciation of the task demands and consequently more successful performances. The design of the training study is shown in Table 6.3.

Table 6.3 Design of training study

A	Pre-training session
	1 Week 1
	2 Week 2
	(4 week gap)
B	Training session
	(Morning)
C	Testing session
	(Afternoon)

6.2.1 Examples of pre- and post-training performances

(9a) Pre-training performance of the pegboard task.

> put a red peg + in the box + anywhere you want + take a yellow peg + go straight along + about ten holes + then take another peg and put it below + the yellow one + about + ten down + and take a yellow green + elastic band + and put it on them + and then + take a blue + + put it + on the board + take another blue + another red put it below + the blue about eleven + twelve down + and take a blue + and put it ten along from the red + then take a red elastic band and join them all up

(9b) Post-training performance of the same speaker on another version of the pegboard task.

> Speaker: put + a red peg + at the bottom + right-hand corner + then about two inches + put a green peg in + then go back to the + red peg + over from the red peg + to your

left + in the middle + it's still in the bottom line put another red peg + then put a green + elastic band over them all + then go to the middle + and a little bit up from the middle + put + a blue + and then + on the top + right-hand corner + about two inches away from that on the very top line + put a blue + about four inches away from that + put a blue + then about three inches down + put a green + then along from the green to your left + at the other side of the board + at the left-hand corner + down from it about + no put it the same + same line as the other green but right at the corner right at the edge of the board + + then put a + red elastic band over them the whole band and then + the blue and the two greens

Hearer: what colour of peg?
Speaker: a green
Hearer: and a red elastic band?
Speaker: aye
Hearer: what three?
Speaker: the blue the blue at the top and the two reds the two greens sorry

(10a) Pre-training performance of the diagram task.
draw with the red pen draw half a square + and then + between the half a square go up to the corner + and draw another square eh with the black pen + and then from the the top right-hand corner of the square draw a red line + + and then draw a black line next to the red one + and then draw a full red square + have you done it? + and then up the very top put a A

(10b) Post-training performance of the same speaker on another version of the diagram task.
at the + the right-hand corner at the bottom go up about three inches and in from the paper about three inches + and when you go up three inches draw a black line about four inches + right you done that? + right get the red pen and draw a square about four by five + right done it? + you've drawn a black line about four inches drawn + a square about the same length as four inches and up five + right you done that? + right about one inch from the square draw a black line about + three inches no two + up the tip of your square + + then about another inch up draw a number five with the red pen + right done it? + that's it

(11a) Pre-training performance of the car crash task.

> There was this + car + on the left-hand side he's turning round to go straight + straight on + + then he's turning too quick and the other car + looks as if it's going straight on + and that pulls out in front of it + and it's going + that is turning up to go up the way and the other guy's going straight down and he brakes + and the other car brakes and the other + + the car at the back of it rams right into the other car

(11b) Post-training performance of the same speaker on another version of the car crash task.

> this red car with the white roof + and it's + going + as it was going along the road + to turn up the way to go up the way + + and there's two cars coming down an orange car with a + it's like a tyre on it yes it's like a big sticker a tyre a big circle and + a white stripe going through it and there's a Ford Capri + a red Ford Capri behind it + and the white the big red car with the white roof + goes round to turn a corner + + and that car with the circle on it it's going straight down with the Capri at its back + and then + that big right + the two of them are + the big red car with the white roof is turning the corner and that other car with the round circle on it is turning in + + and that turns it and takes them by surprise and the + the big + the big white the big red car with the white roof + turns round and takes a a driver doing that orange car + with the circle on it takes him by surprise + and as it turns round the Ford Capri at the back comes smashing right into it.

Although we do not claim that the post-training performances of these speakers are perfect, in all three cases, which are fairly typical of this small group's performances on half a dozen different tasks, the post-training performances do show considerable improvement over the initial performances. If we look first at the pegboard task, which was the 'static' task on which the group was given training, we see that right from the speaker's initial instruction, there are significant differences between the two performances. In (9a), the speaker explicitly abandons responsibility for the task by telling the hearer to put a peg 'anywhere you want'. As this is the very first instruction, it follows that nothing the speaker says after this can result in the hearer being able to reproduce the appropriate pegboard configuration. So although our scoring procedures do not weight the information which a speaker gives or omits to give, such an omission in general terms seems to suggest that this speaker totally fails to appreciate the hearer's requirements in this task. In contrast, in her post-training performance, the speaker correctly orientates her hearer at the beginning of the task and continues to provide throughout the instructions much more information more consistently than in her earlier attempt.

We commented in our experimental studies, in Section 6.1.3 that one effect of hearer experience on subsequent spoken performances, is that speakers include instructions which contain alternative forms of the same information which may be redundant, but add to the general impression that the speaker is really trying to provide the hearer with the maximum amount of information. In (9b) the speaker also does this for example, in saying, 'to your left at the other side of the board at the left-hand corner . . . same line as the other green but right at the corner right at the edge of the board'. The speaker is trying to define a single location with a variety of complementary descriptions to ensure that the hearer knows where to place the peg. Interestingly, the amount of effort the speaker expends on this specification causes her to omit to mention the colour of the peg concerned, but this fault may be one which further practice on the task might overcome. The major achievement which the speaker demonstrates in (9b) is her greater appreciation of the hearer's needs in the task and her ability to use language flexibly and reasonably effectively to transfer the required information.

The performances on the diagram task were of great interest because the training session had only involved the pegboard task, so any improvement in the performances on the diagram task would be evidence that the pupils could generalise insights gained from one task to other tasks of a similar type.

The performances illustrated in (10a) and (10b) suggest that such a generalisation has indeed occurred. The speaker in (10a) shows a lack of a understanding of the need for fully explicit instructions similar to that shown in (9a). However, in (10b), the speaker now includes much more of the required information and exhibits the characteristic opening orienting instructions, and the repeated and paraphrased instructions which, we have suggested, typify the performance of speakers who appreciate their hearer's requirements.

The results so far, suggest that the more informal discussion and practice in the hearer's role which we used in our training session, produced similar improvements in the performances of 'static instructional tasks' to those which we had observed in the experimental manipulations of task conditions. Our next interest was in discovering if similar improvements would occur in the performances of 'dynamic' tasks.

The initial performances of 'dynamic' tasks suggested that it was in car crash descriptions, which demand considerable referential explicitness, that these speakers had the greatest difficulties. (The examples in (11a) and (11b) exemplify typical changes in the performances of these tasks.) We experimented in our training session with a variety of tasks for our group to perform as hearers to attempt to sensitise them to the need for informative and consistent descriptions of the cars. The group tried to select the appropriate pictures being described from pairs of alternatives. They attempted in another performance to draw the accident schematically, and in yet another they attempted to arrange model cars on a layout. This last task, although it led to many insightful and relevant comments and suggestions about the speaker's performance, did expose the pupils to the colours of cars, which were photographed in black and white in the stimulus materials which the speakers were describing.

In the afternoon testing sessions, although the pupils were presented with similar stimuli to those used for the initial pre-training recordings, most of them could remember and use the colours of the model cars in their descriptions – an option which was not available to them in their initial performances. This means the two sets of performances are not strictly comparable: nonetheless the difference in the use of language in the two conditions is sufficiently interesting to include in spite of this factor.

The sheer difference in length between (11a) and (11b) suggests that the speaker in (11b) was demonstrating a much greater concern to try to describe the events accurately and completely. In fact, most of the increased length results from exactly those aspects of the task which our training session had attempted to highlight. The speaker produces extended and discriminating descriptions of the cars concerned and, as in the 'static' tasks, often attempts to refine these descriptions by adding extra information. He introduces one car by saying 'an orange car with a it's like a tyre on it yes it's like a big sticker a tyre a big circle and + a white stripe going through it'. Such extended descriptions hardly ever occur in any of the initial performances we recorded in schools. The speaker in (11b) also seems to realise the importance of later descriptions being as informative and consistent as the introductions. For example in struggling to get to the appropriate description in the following extract 'the the big the big white the big red car with the white roof', the speaker demonstrates an appreciation of the task requirements which is completely lacking in the uninformative choice of expressions used in (11a) such as 'this car', 'the other car', 'it' and 'he'.

This change in performance, following simple training procedures, has been shown to occur in both the 'static' and 'dynamic' tasks. We conclude from this informal study, that the kind of manipulations of the task conditions which resulted in improved performances in our experimental studies, could be adapted for use in the less constrained environment of the classroom.

6.3 Suggested manipulations of task conditions for other task types

The previous studies describe our most extensive investigations of conditions which help speakers produce more effective communications. In this section we mention some other types of task and the initial attempts which we have made to devise beneficial conditions for performing them.

6.3.1 Helpful conditions in co-operative tasks

In Chapter 4, we described one type of task which was rather different from the others. This was a co-operative task where the skills being assessed were two pupils' abilities to co-operate in achieving a task goal. In each case speaker A was to inform speaker B how to draw a route on a map which both of them had copies of. However A's map differed slightly from B's and only A had the route marked on his map. From initial recordings of performances on this task, we found that some of the A speakers were fairly insensitive and unhelpful when B volunteered relevant information, and that some of Bs were not sufficiently assertive at those points in the task where they either had relevant information to share with A, or a lack of information which made complying with their partner's instructions impossible. In our manipulations of the task conditions, we were interested in devising situations which would encourage the speakers to interact more effectively.

In one study of the map task, which we conducted recently with a large group of teenage speakers, we tested the effects on the amount of talk provided in a number of potentially beneficial conditions. In general in our initial recordings we found that the least effective co-operative performances were characterised by very little speech, particularly very little speech contributed by speaker B, so we take 'more talk' to be a rough indication of more exchange of task-related information between speakers. The results from our follow-up study will be discussed in terms of the average number of words produced by each participant in the various task conditions. We are of course aware that increased amount of talk does not *necessarily* indicate more effective co-operation and we are in the process of producing a more sensitive assessment protocol for performances on these tasks, but our initial findings concerning amount of speech seem suggestive and interesting in their own right and so we report them here as signposts to paths which teachers might pursue fruitfully. Among the conditions which we chose to investigate was the effect of prior experience in B's role in the task on subsequent spoken performances. We presented pairs of pupils with four map tasks. In the first two tasks one pupil took A's role and these performances represented the 'no B experience' condition. In the next two tasks, the pupils swapped roles, and As in these tasks represented the 'speakers with B experience' condition. We found that As who had experience of B's role, on average produced nearly twice as much talk as speakers in the A role who had only taken A's role. The extracts shown in the next section illustrate the greater co-operativeness and informativeness of speakers with this prior experience.

The second condition which we investigated focussed on the performance of the pupils in the B role, the subsidiary role. In presenting our pairs of pupils with a series of four map tasks, we included some conditions in which one participant, A, had the complete route shown on his copy of the map and therefore had greater authority in the conduct of the task. In this condition B's role was to contribute information when he either lacked information or had information on his map which was inconsistent with that described by the speaker. In another condition of the task, the route was shown in sections, some of which were on each map. The B speaker in this condition was an equal partner with A and, we supposed, would be forced to contribute a substantial amount of information during the task. The beneficial effect we were interested in testing was whether experience in this role of shared authority would cause B to be more communicative in subsequent performances where A had the complete route and hence greater authority. We compared the amount of speech produced by pupils in B's role who had previous experience in the shared authority condition with the performance of Bs who lacked this experience. We found that the pupils in B's role who had prior experience of shared authority, produced nearly twice as much speech on average in their subsequent performances as Bs without that experience. The extracts below show the kinds of different talk produced by Bs following these two different conditions.

6.3.2 Examples of performances on the co-operative map task

(12) Extract from a performance of a speaker A who has no experience in B's role in the map task.

A: you start + beside the graveyard
B: right

A: go straight up to the volcano + turn right
B: can you slow down?
A: turn right
B: right?
A: uhu + go str - a wee bit down + you come to the giraffes + right
B: right
A: then you turn down + and come to a desert
B: right
A: right you go down + turn left + and go down
B: where to?
A: and you come to a dead tree
B: right
A: then you go up + then come down beside the mountains
B: right

(13) Extract from a performance of a speaker A with prior experience in B's role.
A: have you got a graveyard?
B: yes
A: well go over to the graveyard
B: right
A: go above it just a little bit
B: right
A: have you got a volcano?
B: yes
A: well go from the graveyard right up to the volcano
B: right
A: then + have you got giraffes?
B: yes
A: well go from the volcano + turn right round
B: go right round it + over the smoking?
A: what?
B: over the top + where the smoke is coming out?
A: no + underneath the volcano

If we compare these two performances, we see that there are considerable differences between the way the two speakers, 12A and 13A approach this task. Extract (12) is the complete task performance, while in extract (13) the speaker is only describing the section of the route between two features 'the graveyard' and 'the volcano', a section of route which speaker 12A describes in only a few words in his initial two instructions. This kind of difference obviously results in the overall disparities in the amount of speech which we observed when comparing the two conditions overall. In these examples we can see how the amount of speech produced in this task relates to the degree of effective co-operation which the pupils exhibit. For example, in (12) speaker A not only provides B with minimal information in the instructions about the route, he also apparently provides this information too quickly, and when asked to slow down, only repeats the last of a series of instructions. Later in the task, he completely ignores B's request for more information, and, as a whole, the performance could be described as minimally informative and minimally co-operative.

In contrast, in (13), speaker A regularly checks that his partner has a feature before giving an instruction which uses the feature as a destination. He also gives more detailed information about the location of the route, for example by saying not just that the route goes 'to the graveyard' but that it goes 'above it just a little bit'. This kind of specification, which speaker 12A omits, makes it more likely that B can reproduce the route accurately. Speaker 13A is also more responsive to B's comments, for example when B asks for further specification of a direction, A first indicates that he doesn't understand B's comment and, then, when B expands his question A in turn expands the instruction. This kind of co-operative interchange makes success on the task more likely. The kind of insensitivity which speaker 12A exhibits when he ignores queries from B is likely to decrease the chances for such effective dialogue, both because A does not respond and also because this lack of response is likely to discourage B from further active participation in the task. Experience in B's role again sensitises the speaker to B's point of view in this task and decreases the likelihood that the speaker will adopt such unhelpful and unproductive communication strategies in subsequent tasks.

(14) Extract from a performance on the map task where A has all the information concerning the route to be drawn by B, and the hearer has no prior experience of shared information and authority in this type of task.

A: and you come to a dead tree
B: right
A: then you go up + then come down beside the mountain
B: right

(15) Extract from a performance on the map task where, although in this version of the task A has all the information concerning the route the hearer must draw, B has prior experience in the task having had shared information about the route on an earlier version of the task.

A: turn right across the top of the dead tree + go up a wee bit + across em left + right + across right and down to the finish – have you got that?

B: I've not got the finish + down to the lake?

A: well you know where the lake is?

B: aye

A: go up a wee bit that's where the finish mark is

B: OK I've got that

In these two short extracts the two speakers 14A and 15A are describing how B should draw the end of the route onto their maps. In extract (14), A provides B with a fairly vague description of where to end, 'down beside the mountain', but B does not ask for any expansion of this instruction nor does she ask the speaker to relate this direction to other features which are nearby on her map. This B is exhibiting minimum participation by accepting A's instructions, more or less without comment, even when these instructions are less than fully explicit and where B has relevant information which could be used to seek further specification of the instructions.

In extract (15), B is rather more assertive and, as a result, the final description of where the route has to be drawn is more precise. Speaker 15B, who has exactly the same information on his map as speaker 14B, uses this, namely the feature 'lake' to ask for an alternatie description of an instruction which contains a feature 'the finish', which he does not have. Even in these short examples, we can see that the greater the amount of co-operative dialogue between the participants, the more likely they are to complete the task accurately and successfully. The simple conditions which we offered to our participants, prior shared experience of authority, and prior experience in the subordinate role, seemed to encourage speakers in both roles to exchange more information on the task. If our more detailed examination and assessment of the performances produced in these conditions confirms that more information exchange in general means more effective co-operation, and hence more successful task performances, then these are conditions which can be used in the classroom to encourage pupils to communicate and co-operate successfully in spoken language tasks.

6.3.3 Helpful conditions in 'summary' tasks
The ability to produce a concise summary of an extensive set of information is generally recognised as an important study skill. As we described in Chapter 4, researchers Brown and Day (1983), have investigated some

of the constituent skills involved, such as the ability to delete trivial information and thus select only important information for inclusion in a summary, the ability to substitute a more general description for a list of particular items or events and the ability to select or invent a topic sentence with which to begin a summary. In our initial studies of spoken summaries, we found that many academically less able speakers did not readily deploy these skills and were generally rather unsuccessful at producing concise summaries of even fairly straightforward narrative stimulus material.

We wanted to elicit more effective performances in this important type of task and so we tried to provide more helpful task conditions for the speakers in a second study of summarising skills.

In our earlier study we investigated the effect of offering some speakers the opportunity to tell the whole story shown in the stimulus material early in the recording session, before they were later asked to produce a summary of it. We found that this was the only condition in which we elicited any successful performances of the summary task. Where speakers were asked to look at a set of stimulus photographs and then tell a very short version or summary of the events shown, none of these speakers produced performances which even approached the requested length of 'a three-line summary'. In our later attempts to encourage speakers to produce more effective summaries, we retained the story-summary order of tasks as one probably helpful task condition.

The next observation from our early recordings was that speakers became over-dependent on the stimulus material and, as there were fourteen pictures in the task we had used, they tended to study each one as they told their 'summary'. This meant they included far too much detail in their performances. In our next study we decided to present speakers with the stimulus pictures from which they had already told the complete story, then give the speakers a further opportunity to study the pictures, but finally to remove the stimulus material immediately before the performance of the task. This, we hoped, would encourage the speakers to be more selective about details of the events and would also force the speakers to spend time studying the pictures before beginning their summaries. In the earlier study many speakers were reluctant to spend time on this initial study and preparation.

We also decided to design rather carefully the content of the narratives to be summarised. We found that the only summarising skill, as described by Brown and Day (1983), which some of our speakers exhibited, was the ability to delete some trivial information. In designing narrative stimulus material with a summarising task in mind, we wanted a story which contained a few very salient details. The narrative genre which seemed most appropriate was the murder story, in which we assumed that details such as 'the body', 'the discovery of the killer' and 'the arrest' would seem to be much more important to most people than, for example, trivial details of what an innocent bystander did or said.

The combination of dramatic task content, with its supposed easy selection of important details, prior experience of the story-telling task from the same stimulus material, and the removal of the stimulus material during the summarising task, provided what we hoped would be maximally helpful conditions for the speakers to produce the summary.

The resulting summaries were markedly more successful than those produced in our original study described in Section 4.4.1. The average length of the summaries was around thirty words, so the majority of the performances successfully met the length requirement. The content of the summaries when compared to that of the stories also showed that, in general, speakers were able to select appropriately salient information, although some trivial details were retained. An example of a typical narrative and summary pair are given in Section 6.3.4, and these show that he condition we have devised for this task allow speakers to produce performances which although often faulty, particularly as regards referential explicitness, are nonetheless recognisable summaries. The pupil is demonstrating a skill on which a teacher could build with a wider range of materials.

6.3.4 Examples of murder narrative and summary

(16a) Narrative performance.

> there's a maid and she's got a teapot + and a tray with + food on it + and she walks into a room + and she sees + a lady stabbed + lying in her bed + and + the maid + runs out and phones the police + and tells what she thinks + might have happened + the police come to investigate + and the police are asking questions + to a + lady + the lady is telling what she thinks + happened + + the + maid is now telling + the police + what she thought might have happened + + and what she did + she's saying something else as well + then the policeman brings in a coat with blood on it + and the police thinks it's + the young girl's friend stabbing + the lady + and + the police have caught the girl

(16b) Summary performance.

> the maid + goes into the room and finds that the lady's dead in

her bed + so she phones the police + the police come to investigate + and then the police start asking questions + about what's
happened + to the maid and another girl + and then the police
find the coat and they find out + that the lady + had killed the
lady in bed

6.4 Implications for classroom practice

In this chapter we have described a series of investigations, both systematic and informal, of conditions which can be employed in the task-based
approach to elicit more successful communications from pupils who do
not in general exhibit effective information transferring skills. In a wide
variety of communication tasks, we have found that rather similar, basically simple manipulations of the conditions under which the tasks are
performed, can have significant effects on the speakers' chances of performing the tasks successfully. We believe that the teacher can maximise
a pupil's chance of success on a given task by presenting it in the most
helpful conditions. Pupils perform most effectively when they are communicating with another pupil who is trying to complete some understood task which depends on the speaker's clear and careful transfer of
information. The speaker performs best when given prior experience
both in speaking on the task and, more importantly, in taking the
hearer's role. This combined experience sensitises the speaker to the
hearer's requirements and encourages the speaker to be more explicitly
informative. The tasks should also be presented to speakers in ascending
order of difficulty, whether within a particular type of task, by presenting easier versions first, or between task types, by presenting easier task
types such as narratives before summaries. These are the beneficial conditions which we have found to have an effect across a variety of different
types of task.

We have also found some helpful conditions specific to a particular
type of task such as removing the stimulus material during the summarising task, and providing experience of shared authority in a co-operative
task. There must be many more specific and generally helpful conditions
which the teacher will discover when creating and teaching a course on
developing spoken language skills.

The conditions we have discovered may provide the teacher with a useful starting point when considering such teaching. The effects we have
reported occured both in experimental and informal settings. The
improvements we observed in speakers' performances were fairly substantial, and, as we have shown, the effects lasted over time. The insights

which speakers gained following helpful conditions provided in one task, also led to improvement in the performances of other similar tasks. The size, duration and generalisability of the beneficial effects of the task conditions which we report here, suggest that these are useful resources which the teacher could apply in the classroom.

We hope that these findings will encourage the teacher to seek other conditions which could be manipulated to help the pupils demonstrate the kind of progress we have evidence that they are capable of making in oral communication skills. The performances we have recorded suggest that many teenage speakers are initially less than fully effective in communicating information but also, more positively, that with the aid of the right conditions, and help from discussions and teachers, they can demonstrate real progress in this area.

6.5 Conclusion

We have tried, in this book, to contribute to the growing discussion of what it might mean to take seriously the teaching of the spoken language in schools. We have deliberately limited our discussion. We have largely ignored aspects of the spoken language which are often discussed – fluency, pronunciation, choice of vocabulary, rhetorical style, self-presentation. We have ignored many aspects of teaching the spoken language which interest many teachers – self-expression, drama, the ability to chair committees, participate in debates, and so on. We do not suggest that these areas are unimportant, on the contrary. It is because they are so important that they are all relatively well-known and well-discussed. We have chosen to concentrate on an area that seems to us extremely important but, for some curious reason, overlooked. We have concentrated on the ability to transfer information clearly. We believe that this ability is relevant not only for speaking but also for writing. Indeed, we believe that it is fundamental to the whole process of education, echoing the words of a nineteenth-century scholar:

They who are learning to compose and arrange their sentences with accuracy and order, are learning, at the same time, to think with accuracy and order.
(Lindley Murray, *English grammar adapted to different classes of learners*)

Appendix A Descriptions and illustrations of the tasks

1 Examples of tasks involving static relationships

1.1 The diagram-drawing task

In this task, the speaker has a diagram which the hearer cannot see. The hearer has a blank sheet of paper, a red pen and a black pen. The speaker has to provide the hearer with detailed instructions on how to reproduce the diagram as accurately as possible.

This task requires that the speaker provides the hearer with clear descriptions about a series of entities which have to be drawn, such as lines, squares and numbers, the relevant properties of these entities such as size, shape and colour, and the spatial relationships which hold between them.

Examples of adequate and less than adequate performances on this task are given in Chapters 4, 5, and 6. Scoring protocols for performances on this task are shown in Appendix B.

This task can readily be made more or less difficult for the speaker, depending on the number of entities included in any particular diagram, and the nature of the spatial relationships which exist between them. Figures 1a, 1b and 1c show diagram-drawing task stimuli which we have used extensively and which we have found represent three ascending levels of difficulty for teenage speakers. We call these the easy, intermediate and difficult versions of the diagram task.

Figure 1a Diagram-drawing task, easy level

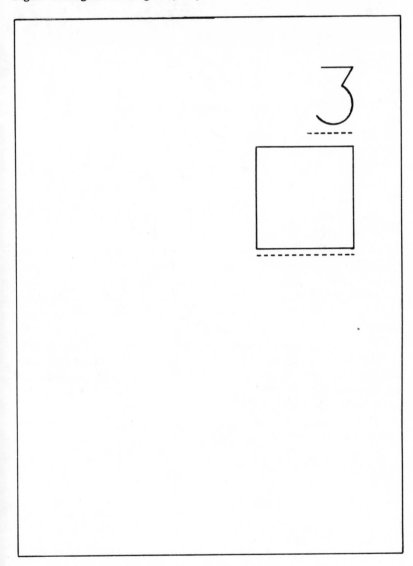

Note: ———— indicates black lines, – – – indicates red lines.
Original diagrams 12×8 inches.

Figure 1b Diagram-drawing task, intermediate level

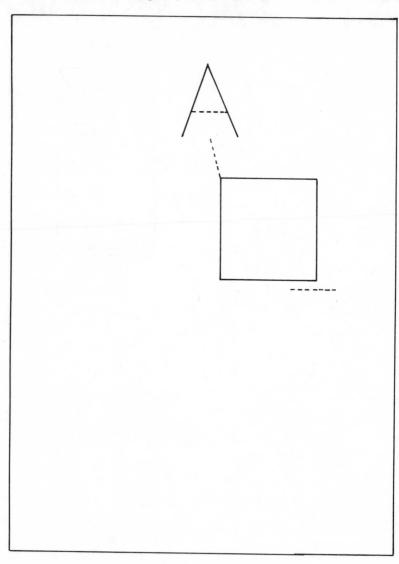

Note: ———— indicates black lines, – – – indicates red lines.

Figure 1c Diagram-drawing task, difficult level

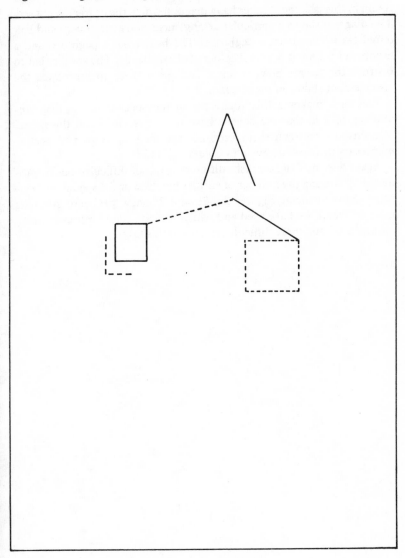

Note: ——— indicates black lines, – – – indicates red lines.

1.2 The pegboard task

Again in this task the speaker has a diagram which the hearer cannot see. The diagram shows a particular arrangement of coloured pegs and coloured elastic bands on a pegboard. The hearer has a pegboard and a number of coloured pegs and coloured elastic bands. The speaker has to instruct the hearer how to select and place these to reproduce the arrangement shown in the diagram.

This task makes similar demands of the speaker to the diagram-drawing task in that the objects have to be described and the spatial relationships between them carefully specified. Examples of performances on this task are given in Chapters 5 and 6.

Again like the diagram task, different levels of difficulty can be produced by altering the number of entities involved or the spatial relationships between them. Figures 2a, 2b and 2c show pegboard stimulus material which we have used and which we have found represent easy, intermediate and more difficult versions of this task.

Figure 2a Pegboard task, easy level

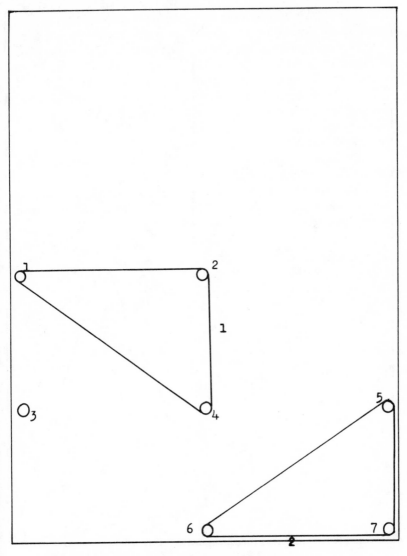

Note: ○ indicates coloured pegs, ——— coloured elastic bands.
    Numbers did not appear on the original, but refer to the scoring protocol in
    Chapter 5.
    Original diagrams 8×6 inches.

Figure 2b Pegboard task, intermediate level

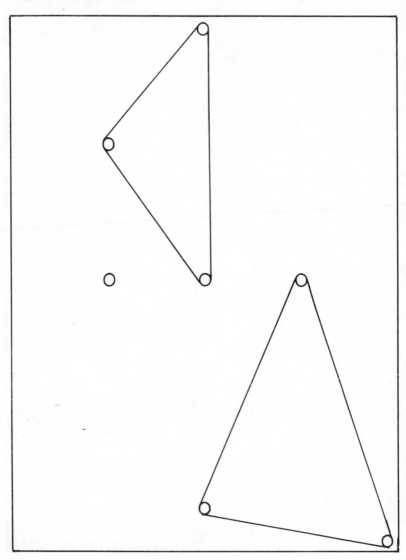

Note: ○ indicates coloured pegs, ——— indicates coloured elastic bands.

Figure 2c Pegboard task, difficult level

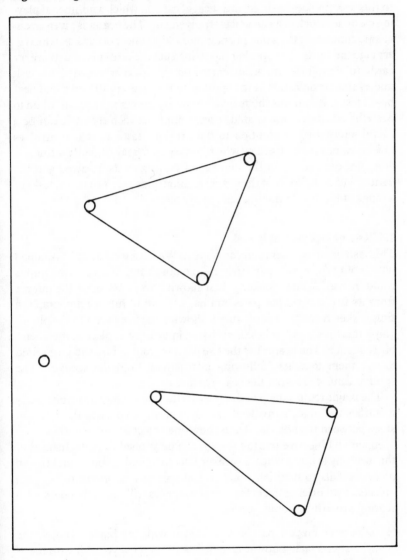

Note: ○ indicates coloured pegs, ——— indicates coloured elastic bands.

1.3 The playing cards task

In this task the speaker is given a sheet of card on which a number of playing cards are stuck in a particular arrangement. The hearer is given an envelope containing the same playing cards and a sheet of card on which to arrange the cards. The speaker has to instruct the hearer how to place his cards to reproduce the arrangement on the speaker's card. This task makes similar demands of the speaker to the diagram-drawing and pegboard tasks. It requires the speaker to specify the cards in question and to describe accurately the spatial relationships between them. It can be a useful alternative or addition to the previous tasks in that it involves objects rather than diagrams which some pupils may find offputting.

Again, depending on the number of playing cards involved and the variety and complexity of the spatial relationships between them, tasks of a range of levels of difficulty can readily be produced.

1.4 The object assembly task

This task involves assembling an object. (We have used an old-fashioned household mincer but any fairly simple object not known to the pupils could be used.) The speaker is first shown how to assemble the mincer from its five component parts and has in front of him a photograph (a simple sketch could be substituted) showing the five parts. In the photograph there is a number beside each part indicating its place in the assembly sequence. The hearer has the five parts in front of him and is required to put them together, following instructions from the speaker. The speaker cannot see what the hearer is doing.

The major requirement of such tasks is that the speaker unambiguously identifies the objects involved and then clearly expresses the relationships between the objects, that is, how one object fits into another.

Again an objective scoring system can be applied to performances of this task, by scoring when a speaker fails to unambiguously identify an object or fails to mention some crucial part of a relationship between objects. Two brief extracts from performances will illustrate how such a scoring procedure would operate.

(1) take your biggest part + and hold it with the biggest ring + the widest end facing upwards to the roof + and get your bit with the + ken like a screw + and + put it in with the square end at the bottom

(2) the part that looks like a gun that's the first one + then you've got the second part's a drill + + and then you fit it in

In both extracts the objects involved are adequately identified and the basic relationship between them expressed. However, in the second description, the speaker gives no indication of *how* the second object fits into the first, although the task clearly requires that this should be mentioned. The scoring system can reflect such differences between performances.

A series of object assembly tasks of different levels of difficulty can be produced either by using different objects which involve more or fewer constituent parts with simple or more complicated relationships between them, or by having an object which has stages in its assembly which can initially be tackled separately and then later attempted as a whole.

The advantage which this type of task offers is that it encourages speakers to use the language they have constructively. There is no correct vocabulary which is generally available to identify the constituent parts of objects, the speaker has to construct his own. The task also has good face validity for speakers: the object can only be assembled if he provides good clear instructions and this is readily demonstrable by examining the object which the hearer has assembled or failed to assemble and comparing the tape of the speaker's instructions with any problems in the assembly of the object.

2 Examples of tasks involving dynamic relationships

2.1 The narrative tasks

In these tasks, the speaker is presented with a series of line drawings and is asked to tell the story which they illustrate, to another pupil.

The hearer is given a task to perform while the story is being related, such as arranging a series of pictures from the story into the correct order, or identifying which of a number of drawn characters appear in the story. The speaker is not told, nor can he see, the hearer's task. However, the speaker is informed that the success of the task depends on the hearer's correct understanding of the story.

Examples of speakers' performances on one particular narrative task which we have used extensively are given in Chapters 4, 5 and 6. The first three (of fourteen) stimulus pictures for this task are shown in Figures 3a, b and c.

As described in Chapter 4, narrative tasks make four main demands on speakers: (a) the speaker must be referentially explicit in his use of language, that is he must clearly indicate which characters or objects are involved at a particular point in the story; (b) the speaker must clearly describe the main activities or events which occur in the story; (c) the

Figure 3a Narrative task, first stimulus picture

Figure 3b Narrative task, second stimulus picture

Figure 3c Narrative task, third stimulus picture

speaker must indicate when any significant changes in time occur, and (d) when any significant changes in location take place.

All narrative tasks will not be equally demanding in all four respects. The narrative task partly illustrated in Figures 3a, b and c, for example, involves only two potentially confusing characters, i.e. two characters who are female, and thus is not very referentially demanding. This narrative does require two changes in location to be indicated but does not require any particular reference to changes in time. If we consider grading narrative tasks in terms of difficulty we have to describe each task in terms of these separate requirements. For example, another narrative task which we have used features a shoplifting incident involving four female characters. This task is more difficult in terms of the need for referential explicitness, but as the events in the story occur in a single location at one period of time, it is less difficult in these respects than the previous task.

In Chapters 5 and 6, we exemplify performances of a murder story, which involves three female characters and thus is of intermediate difficulty in respect to referential explicitness, but makes considerable demands on the speaker to keep the time of the described events clear, as the story involves several 'flashbacks' to critical moments in time.

Speakers should attempt a range of narrative tasks which make different demands. Problems with a particular narrative requirement can be noted and further opportunities to attempt a narrative involving a particular demand can be offered to the pupil.

2.2 The car crash task

In this task speakers are presented with a folder containing four black and white photographs showing the events leading up to a road accident involving model cars. The following instructions were read to the speaker by the experimenter. 'In this folder there are photographs of a car crash which we made up using model cars. I want you to act as if these photographs were taken during a real car crash – and you were an eye witness to this real car crash. You have to describe to your partner how the crash happened as clearly as you can, as if you were reporting the accident to the police. Remember to include as much detail as you can, so that your partner will know exactly how the crash happened.'

The speaker was then told to open the folder and study the pictures carefully before beginning his description. The photographs remained in front of the speaker throughout the task.

The hearer was also handed a folder containing photographs. In this case there were three pairs of photographs representing alternative beginnings, middles and ends for a car crash. The hearer was given the following written instructions: 'The speaker is going to describe a car crash. You have to choose the correct picture for the *start, middle* and *end* of the description. Put a tick beside the picture you choose. Don't ask your partner any questions.'

Both speaker and hearer were given an opportunity to ask questions about the task before they began, and the experimenter generally tried to make sure that all subjects understood the task, by repeating or rephrasing the instructions.

As in the narrative tasks, the major requirement for success in the car crash task is that the speaker is referentially explicit in his use of language to introduce and subsequently to refer to the vehicles involved in the crash. An adequate description also requires that the speaker conveys adequate information about the physical location and temporal ordering of the events leading up to the accident.

Car crash tasks of various degrees of difficulty can readily be produced by altering the number and discriminability of the vehicles involved. For example, we found a higher degree of referential success was achieved by speakers who described a crash involving a car and a lorry, than by speakers describing an accident involving three fairly similar-looking cars.

The task can be separately graded for difficulty depending on the complexity of the spatial relationships involved. All our examples cited in Chapters 5 and 6 involve accidents which occurred at crossroads, thus the cars involved were in a fairly complex spatial layout. Simpler tasks would involve either a junction or a straight road.

Figure 4a Car crash task, first stimulus picture

Figure 4b Car crash task, second stimulus picture

Figure 4c Car crash task, third stimulus picture

Figure 4d Car crash task, fourth stimulus picture

Appendix B
Assessment protocols

1.1 Teachers' assessment of narratives, 'structured' versus 'unstructured' scoring

Shown below are the instructions and one sample scoring protocol given to teachers who participated in the first assessment study described in Chapter 5. No title appeared on the sheets originally used in the experiment.

Narrative task 'structured' scoring instructions

<u>Time allowed: 10 minutes</u>   Name:_____

You are asked to listen to five tape-recorded accounts of what happened in a piece of film and to provide a score *out of ten* as your assessment of how 'good' you think each account is.

The assessment method you are asked to use is presented on the following pages as a set of ten marks to be awarded to each account. Award *one* mark each time the information beside a box is clearly and unambiguously expressed in the speaker's account.

Concentrate on identifying *WHO DID WHAT*. The account of the sequence of events is a success if you are sure throughout about *WHO* was involved in each event, *WHAT* the events were, and the simple relationships between the participants and the events.

Note:

1 You are *not* being asked to award marks for specific vocabulary. The speaker does not have to use the word 'escape', for example.
   What is important is that the speaker describes the action, by using the word 'escape' or any other that is appropriate.

2 It is important that the participants should be adequately identified and *distinguished from each other*. Only award marks if you are *sure* which participant is involved in each event.

If you have any brief comments to make on your assessment procedure, please provide them below:

Narrative task 'structured' scoring protocol

1 ☐ Character A . . .   escaping from/ . . .   ropes/chains/a straitjacket
                            getting out of

2 ☐ Character B . . .   breaking into/ . . .   cars
                            stealing things from

3 ☐ Marking simultaneous action . . .   as/while/ . . .   B stealing
                                            meanwhile   while A
                                                                   escaping

4 ☐ Character B (distinctly identified)

5 ☐ . . . steals a camera

6 ☐ Character A (distinctly identified)

7 ☐ . . . gets out of the ropes, etc.

8 ☐ Character B (distinctly identified)

9 ☐ . . . takes a photo of

10 ☐ . . . Character A (distinctly identified)

Narrative task 'unstructured' scoring instructions

<u>Time allowed: 10 minutes</u>   Name:_____

You are asked to listen to five tape-recorded accounts of what happened in a piece of film and to provide a score *out of ten* as your assessment of how 'good' you think each account is.

Use whatever criteria you think are appropriate as the basis of your assessment.

If you can identify those aspects of the speaker's spoken English account which influenced your assessment, describe them briefly in the 'Comments' section at the bottom of the page.

Speaker 1:   /10

Speaker 2:   /10

Speaker 3:   /10

Speaker 4:   /10

Speaker 5:   /10

Comments:

1.2 Teachers' assessments of diagram instructions, 'structured' versus 'unstructured' scoring

Shown below are the instructions and scoring protocols given to teachers who participated in the first assessment study described in Chapter 5. The teachers were randomly assigned to two groups; one group scored the narrative task using the structured scoring protocols, and the diagram-drawing task using the unstructured scoring procedure. The other group used structured scoring protocols to assess the diagram instructions and unstructured procedures to score the narratives. Each group used the unstructured procedure before the structured one. No headings appeared on the original materials given to teachers.

Diagram-drawing task, 'unstructured' scoring instructions

Time allowed: 20 minutes   Name:_____

On this section of tape there are five recordings of teenagers giving instructions on how to draw a particular diagram. Each speaker has the diagram in front of him and has to instruct a listener who has a blank sheet of paper and coloured pens but who does not know what the diagram is like.

You have to provide a score *out of ten* as your assessment of how 'good' you think each description is.

Use whatever criteria you think are appropriate as the basis of your assessment.

If you can identify those aspects of the speaker's spoken English description which influenced your assessment, describe them briefly in the 'Comments' section at the bottom of the page. Please *do not replay* any piece of tape *more than three* times.

Speaker 1:   /10

Speaker 2:   /10

Speaker 3:   /10

Speaker 4:   /10

Speaker 5:   /10

Comments:

Diagram-drawing task, 'structured' instructions

<u>Time allowed: 20 minutes</u>   Name:_____

READ INSTRUCTIONS CAREFULLY *BEFORE* PLAYING TAPE

On this section of tape there are five recordings of teenagers giving instructions on how to draw a particular diagram. Each speaker has the diagram in front of him and has to instruct a listener who has a blank sheet of paper and coloured pens but who does not know what the diagram is like. Your task is to score how well each speaker gives his instructions. Listed below are twenty items of information which the speaker should provide; you have to tick each item mentioned by a speaker *while* you are listening to each piece of tape.

For example, a speaker might begin by saying 'At the top put a large number three'. You would tick the boxes marked TOP, THREE and SIZE but you should leave the boxes marked RIGHT and COLOUR blank, as the speaker has not said anything about the 'three' being on the top *right* of the page nor about the colour of the 'three'. Speakers may give sizes or distances in terms of actual measurements by inches or centimetres, in general terms or in relation to any previously mentioned item, in all cases you should tick the appropriate box, e.g. 'A big box' and 'A square two inches' would both get ticks for SQUARE and SIZE as would 'A square bigger than the red line'. Any type of mention of size is scored with a tick in the appropriate box.

The boxes are ordered in a logical sequence, so for example in

THREE   ☐

SIZE   ☐

COLOUR ☐

the size and colour boxes refer to any mention of the colour or size of the number three in the diagram. However, speakers do not always provide the information in sequence and marks are still scored (by ticking boxes) for information provided at any stage of the instructions.

Remember please, tick the appropriate boxes *while* you are listening to the tape, *not afterwards* and *do not replay* any piece of tape *more than three times*.

Diagram-drawing task 'structured' scoring protocol

	Speaker A	Speaker B	Speaker C	Speaker D	Speaker E
Top					
Right					
Three					
Size					
Colour					
Down/Under/Below					
Distance					
Line					
Colour					
Size					
Down/Under/Below					
Distance					
Square/Box					
Colour					
Size					
Down/Under/Below					
Distance					
Line					
Colour					
Size					

2.1 Teachers' assessment of car crash task

Shown below are the instructions to teachers who partcipated in the second assessment study described in Chapter 5, followed by a sample scoring protocol.

Accompanying this sheet there are three assessment exercises plus a cassette tape. On the cassette, there are examples of the speech of 15–16 year-old pupils from Scottish schools.

1 The first assessment exercise is detailed on the set of sheets marked 'Car crash descriptions'. Read over the first page for a few minutes. On *side A* of the cassette, there are 5 examples of car crash descriptions. Listen to these descriptions and carry out the exercise according to the directions.

Total time taken in reading the directions, listening to the 5 taped examples and putting ticks on the speakers' sheets should not exceed *20 minutes*.

Car crash descriptions   Name:_____

In this task, speakers were asked to provide an eye witness account of a car crash, for a hearer who had not been present when the car crash took place.

On the accompanying tape there are five of these eye witness accounts. You are asked to listen to the five accounts and assess how effectively the speaker has described what happened.

The assessment procedure you are asked to use is presented on the following pages. For each speaker there is a page which shows 3 possible layouts for the beginning of the description, 3 layouts for the middle, and 3 layouts for the end. You have to choose one of the 3 layouts for each part according to the description you hear on the tape for each speaker.

So, you should listen to the tape of speaker 1, and put three ticks ($\sqrt{}$), one in the box beside the 'beginning' layout you think the speaker is describing, one beside the 'middle' layout you choose, and one beside the 'end' layout you choose.

Only put a tick beside the 'Don't know' box if you are totally unsure about what is being described.

Do not spend a long time on this exercise. You should complete the exercise after listening to the tape twice through. Do not spend more than *15 minutes* on the exercise.

Do you have any (brief) comments to make on this assessment exercise?

Beginning of description (Choose one)

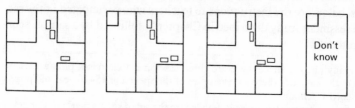

Middle of description (Choose one)

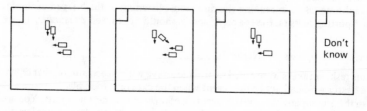

End of description (Choose one)

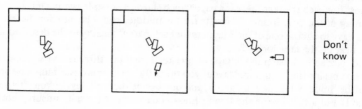

2.2 Teachers' assessments of story beginnings and opinions
Shown below are the instructions to teachers who participated in the second assessment study. The instructions concern two assessment tasks, one concerned with how speakers begin stories, the other with how well speakers express an opinion. Scoring protocols for both assessment exercises are shown.

The second assessment exercise involves 'Story beginnings' and a separate sheet contains directions and a scoring table. On *side B* of the cassette, there are 6 examples of 'story beginnings'. Listen to these extracts and carry out the exercise according to the directions.

Total time taken should not exceed *10 minutes*.

The third assessment exercise involves 'Opinions on the Belt', and a separate sheet contains directions and a scoring table. On the second part of *side B* of the cassette, there are 6 examples of 'Belt opinions'. Listen to these extracts and carry out the exercise according to the directions.

Total time taken should not exceed *15 minutes*.

Exercise in assessing spoken English

Name:_____

In this exercise, speakers were asked to look over a set of line drawings which formed a story-sequence and then to tell the story, as if they were telling a friend what happened. The first two line drawings of the sequence are reproduced below as picture 1 and picture 2.

On the accompanying tape are six versions of how speakers began their accounts, based on the two line drawings presented.

You are asked to listen to the six versions and assess how well you think the speaker has begun his/her account.

The assessment method you are asked to use is presented as a set of 8 marks to be awarded to each account. Put a tick ($\checkmark$), in the appropriate box, each time the information beside one of the numbers is clearly expressed in the speaker's account.

(See Appendix A, Figures 3a and 3b.)

Details to be scored	*Speakers*					
	A	B	C	D	E	F
1 location ('house'/'living room')						
2 male character ('a man'/'husband')						
3 his activity ('sitting'/'smoking')						
4 his state ('bored'/'fed up')						
5 female character ('a woman'/'wife')						
6 her activity ('sitting'/'reading')						
7 male character ('he'/'the man')						
8 his activity ('goes to window')						

Do you have any (brief) comments to make on this assessment exercise?

Exercise in assessing spoken English

Name:_____

A group of pupils were shown a film in which a man was sitting behind a desk with a belt (a tawse) in his hand. The man stated that, in his opinion, the belt was necessary in Scottish schools. At the beginning of the cassette tape which *you* have, the spoken version of this film can be heard.

After they had watched the film, the pupils were asked the question: 'What do you think about that?'

On *your* tape, there are six different responses to this question.

In this assessment exercise, you are asked to listen to the six responses and assign a grade, A, B, or C to each response. The criteria for these grades are presented on the right-hand side of the page.

Speaker	Grade Assigned (A, B, or C)
1	
2	
3	
4	
5	
6	

Grade C = opinion expressed
   but *no* reason given
   and *no* alternative considered

Grade B = opinion expressed
   plus a reason given
   but *no* alternative considered

Grade A = opinion expressed
   plus a reason given
   plus an alternative considered

If you have any comments on this assessment procedure, please write them in the space provided below:

Appendix C Technical details of experiments

1 Assessment of task performances

1.1 Assessment of task performances by teachers, first study

In the first assessment study, described in Chapter 5, thirty teachers of English judged five speakers performing a 'narrative' task, and five speakers performing a diagram-drawing task. Fifteen teachers assessed the narrative performances using the 'unstructured' procedures described in Appendix B, and then assessed the diagram-drawing performances using the 'structured' procedures. The other fifteen teachers assessed the same speakers, first the diagram task using the 'unstructured' procedures then the narrative task using the 'structured' procedures. The unstructured procedures were used first because we wished teachers to use their own criteria in this condition for judging how good the performances were and we did not wish them to be influenced by the features which our structured scoring protocols focussed their attention on.

In the narrative task, when using the unstructured protocols, teachers assigned marks out of ten to the five speakers, and these marks were converted into a ranking of the five speakers. Similarly when the group of teachers used the structured scoring protocols, they assigned ticks to each speaker's performance when certain points of information were clearly conveyed. The number of ticks assigned to each speaker was also converted into a ranking of the five speakers for that teacher. Table 1 shows the overall rankings of the same five speakers, by the two groups of teachers using the two methods of assessment, based on the individual rankings derived from each teacher's assessment.

Table 1 Teachers' assessments of narrative performances

Group 1 _Teachers using 'unstructured' scoring_		Group 2 _Teachers using 'structured' scoring_
Speaker number 2 'best' performance		Speaker number 3
5		4
3		1
4		2
1 'worst' performance		5

In order to assess the consensus among the teachers' assessments, Kendall's coefficients of concordance (W) were calculated on the basis of each teacher's ranking of the five speakers. In the unstructured condition, $W = .33$, $p< .001$, in the structured condition, $W = .84$, $p< .001$. Thus for the narrative task there was a significant degree of agreement among the teachers in both conditions (although as Table 1 shows they agreed on different rankings in the two conditions). The degree of consensus appears to be greater in the structured condition.

Similar procedures were applied to the teachers' assessments of the diagram performances. Table 2 shows the average rankings of the same five speakers, under the two scoring procedures.

Table 2 Teachers' assessments of diagram performances

Group 1	Group 2
Teachers using 'structured' protocols	*Teachers using 'unstructured' protocols*
Speaker number 5 'best' performance	Speaker number 2
3	3
2	5
1	1
4 'worst' performance	4

Kendall's coefficients of concordance were again calculated to assess consensus in the two groups. For the structured condition, $W = .84$, $p < .001$, and for the unstructured condition, $W = .71$, $p < .001$, which again shows a significant degree of agreement within each group of teachers and again apparently greater consensus in the structured condition.

1.2 Assessment of task performances by teachers, second study

Thirty principal teachers of English participated in the second assessment study described in Chapter 5, using the scoring procedures shown in Appendix B. One of the tasks which the teachers assessed was the way five speakers described the car crash photographs. As the scoring protocols show, the teachers had to decide which of three possible layouts the speaker was describing at the beginning, in the middle, and at the end, of the account of the crash. There was also a 'don't know' box if the teacher could not make such a decision at any stage based on the speaker's description.

We compared the thirty teachers' assessments for each of the five speakers. The percentages of agreement which were calculated are shown in Table 3. The letters refer to the layout which most of the teachers agreed that speaker was describing at that point in the account of the crash. The letters in brackets refer to the layout which was originally presented to the speaker to describe, and so represents what the speaker should have been clearly describing. Chi square tests were performed on the teachers' judgments to test if these differed significantly from a random distribution across the possible categories, a single asterisk denotes a distribution significantly different from chance at the $p < .01$ level, two asterisks denotes $p < .001$.

Table 3 Teachers' assessments of car crash descriptions

	Layout selected by most teachers		
	Beginning	*Middle*	*End*
Speaker 1	A (C)	C (A)	A (B)
% Agreement	100% **	100% **	97% **
Speaker 2	C (A)	C (B)	A (B)
% Agreement	73% **	77% **	33%
Speaker 3	Don't Know (B)	Don't Know (C)	A (A)
% Agreement	33%	47% *	43%
Speaker 4	Don't Know (C)	Don't Know (B)	Don't Know (A)
% Agreement	53% **	50% **	53% **
Speaker 5	B (B)	C (C)	B (B)
% Agreement	93% **	97% **	100% **

Thus twelve out of fifteen judgments by teachers show a significant consensus, but only one of these speakers, Speaker 5, clearly conveys the appropriate description.

The thirty teachers also assessed how much information six speakers included at the beginning of a story-telling performance. The teachers used the assessment protocols shown in Apendix B. The number of points of information ticked for all six speakers was totalled and a ranking of the six speakers by each teacher was calculated. Table 4 shows the consensus ranking of the speakers by all thirty teachers, with the percentage of agreement shown in brackets. A Kendall's coefficient of concordance (W) was calculated based on the ranking of the speakers by individual teachers, to test if the degree of consensus was statistically significant. The result, $W = .61$, $p < .001$, showed a highly reliable agreement among the teachers in this study.

Table 4 Teachers' assessment of information content of speakers' story beginnings

	Consensus ranking	% of agreement
Speaker 1	3	(73%)
2	1	(83%)
3	5	(50%)
4	4	(57%)
5	2	(50%)
6	6	(37%)

2 Results and analyses of experiments

2.1 The effect on the performance of 'static' tasks of practice in speaking and experience in the hearer's role

In Chapter 6 we discussed two experiments which we conducted to test the effects on speakers' performances of 'static' tasks of practice in speaking and experience in the hearer's role.

In the first experiment, we compared the performances of two groups of speakers in two sessions, one week apart. Only one group had experience in the hearer's role between sessions one and two. The mean scores on the tasks for each speaker in the two groups at the two sessions were subjected to analysis of variance. There was a main effect of session ($F\,1, 14 = 11.2$, $p<.01$), with second session performances averaged across both groups, producing higher scores than those on first sessions. There was no main effect of group ($F<1$); that means there was no difference between the scores for the two groups of speakers averaged across the two sessions. There was a significant interaction between session and groups of speakers, ($F\,3,14 = 3.61$, $p<.05$). Within this interaction, planned comparison tests showed that there was no significant difference between the scores for session one and session two for speakers with no experience in the hearer's role (60% versus 62%) but there was a statistically significant ($p<.05$) improvement in the performances of speakers with experience in the hearer's role between session one and two (58% versus 78%).

2.2 The effect on the performance of 'static' tasks of experience in the hearer's role, task difficulty and task order

In the second experiment, which involved forty-nine subjects, the effect on performances of 'static' tasks of practice in the hearer's role was tested along with the effect of task difficulty and the effect of task order. The design of the experiment is shown in Table 5.

Table 5 Design of experiment to test the effects of experience in the hearer's role, task difficulty and task order

	Speaker condition	**Level of difficulty and task order**
Group 1	Speakers without experience of hearer's role	Easy then intermediate tasks
Group 2	Speakers without experience of hearer's role	Intermediate then easy tasks
Group 3	Speakers with experience of hearer's role	Easy then intermediate tasks
Group 4	Speakers with experience of hearer's role	Intermediate then easy tasks

The mean scores for each subject performing both easy and intermediate tasks were subjected to a mixed model three-way analysis of variance treating subjects as a random effect, speaker condition and task order as fixed effects, and level of difficulty as a fixed effect repeated measure.

The analysis showed the following significant effects: first a main effect of speaker condition, (F 1, 45 = 9.83, p<.005), with speakers with hearer experience producing higher scoring performances (75% versus 62% of the required information). The analysis also showed a main effect of task difficulty, (F 1, 45 = 15.9, p<.005), with higher scores on easy tasks compared to intermediate level tasks (74% versus 64% of the required information). There was no main effect of task order. There was a significant interaction between task difficulty and task order, (F 1, 45 = 37.9, p<.001). Within this interaction, planned comparison tests showed that intermediate level tasks which were presented first to subjects result in significantly lower scores, than when either intermediate or easy tasks are the second task a subject tackles. (58% of the required information versus 74% and 79% respectively.)

The triple interaction of speaker condition, task order and task difficulty was also found to be significant, (F 1, 45 = 5.18, p<.05). Within this interaction, planned comparison tests showed several significant differences. These are shown, along with the mean scores for the various experimental conditions, in Table 6.

Table 6 Significant differences (in the % of required information provided by speakers) within the speaker condition × task order × task difficulty interaction

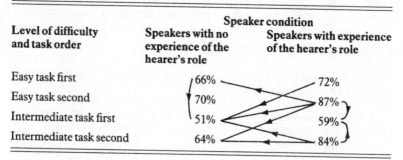

Level of difficulty and task order	Speaker condition	
	Speakers with no experience of the hearer's role	Speakers with experience of the hearer's role
Easy task first	66%	72%
Easy task second	70%	87%
Intermediate task first	51%	59%
Intermediate task second	64%	84%

Arrows indicate those differences found to be statistically significant, and the direction of the difference.

2.3 The effect of practice on the amount of information included by speakers in narratives

In this experiment, twenty-five speakers were recorded telling a story based on fourteen cartoon pictures, on two occasions, one week apart. The stories were transcribed and analysed for the amount of detail they contained. The details depicted in the stimulus material were simply set out as a list of sixty-seven points and one mark was awarded each time one of the details was mentioned in a speaker's story. A t-test for correlated data was performed on the pairs of scores for each speaker from sessions one and two (t 1, 24= 2.81, p < .05). This showed that the average number of details provided by speakers was greater on their second telling of the story (an average of 41 details versus 36 details, respectively).

2.4 The effect of practice and experience in the hearer's role on referential success in the car crash task

To study the effect of practice and experience in the hearer's role, on referential success, we presented fifty-four speakers with two car crashes to describe. (In Appendix A, the task itself is described in detail.) For each speaker we had two performances to compare. Half the speakers only had experience of speaking and half the speakers also had experience in the hearer's role. Each speaker was presented with stimulus photographs which for one task contained two cars or two vehicles, and for the other contained three cars or three vehicles. The performances were recorded, transcribed and then scored for referential success. Individual expressions used by the speaker to refer to one of the vehicles, were judged as successful or unsuccessful using the criteria described in Chapter 6. For each performance an overall percentage of referential success was then calculated based on the number of successful expressions used, compared to the total number of expressions which a speaker used to refer to the vehicles.

This data was subjected to a three-factor analysis of variance, with type of stimulus received by groups of speakers, (3 car, 2 car, 3 vehicle and 2 vehicle) and speaker group (speakers with and without experience in the hearer's role) as between subject grouping factors, and with practice (first task and second task) as a repeated measure within subjects.

The analysis showed a main effect of speaker group, ($F\ 1, 45 = 10.39$, $p < .005$), with speakers with experience in the hearer's role having higher referential success, (77% versus 59%).

There was a significant effect of practice, ($F\ 1, 45 = 4.51$, $p < .05$), with second performances being more successful (73% versus 62% of referential success).

There was a significant triple interaction of type of stimulus received by groups of speakers $\times$ speaker group $\times$ practice, ($F\ 3, 45 = 7.95$, $p < .001$). By using planned comparison tests within this interaction, we were able to compare the effect of type of stimulus on success rates. Three-car tasks were less successful than two-car tasks, ($p < .05$), there was a trend ($.05 < p < .1$) for three-vehicle crashes to be less successful than two-vehicle ones, and three-car descriptions were less successful than two-vehicle descriptions, ($p < .05$). Although the speaker group (speakers with and without experience of the hearer's role) $\times$ practice interaction was not statistically significant, ($F\ 3, 45 = 1.04$), planned comparison tests showed that only speakers with experience of the hearer's role improved between first and second performances ($p < .05$, success rate of 85% versus 68%) and that only these second performances were significantly better than those of speakers without experience of the hearer's role, ($p < .05$).

References

Anderson, A.H. (forthcoming). 'Successful reference', *Journal of Semantics*

Anderson, A.H., Yule, G. & Brown, G. (forthcoming). 'Hearer-effects on speaker performances', *First Language*

Bereiter, C. & Englemann, S. 1966. *Teaching disadvantaged children in the pre-school*. Prentice Hall

Bernstein, B. 1959. 'A public language: some sociological implications of a linguistic form', *British Journal of Sociology*, 10, 311–326

Brown, A.L. & Day, J.D. 1983. 'Macro rules for summarising texts: The development of expertise', *Journal of Verbal Learning and Verbal Behaviour*, 22, 1–14

Brown, G. & Yule, G. 1983. *Teaching the spoken language*. Cambridge University Press

Bullock Report 1975. *A Language for life*. HMSO

Dickson, W.P. 1980. 'Referential communication activities in research and in the curriculum: a meta-analysis' in Dickson W.P. (ed.), *Children's oral communication skills*. Academic Press

Dunning Report 1977. *Assessment for All: A Report of the Committee to Review Assessment in the Third and Fourth Years of Secondary Education in Scotland*. SED/HMSO

Edwards, J.R. 1979. *Language and disadvantage*. Edward Arnold

Labov, W. 1973. 'The logic of non-standard English' in Keddie, N. (ed.), *Tinker, tailor . . . The myth of cultural deprivation*. Penguin

Munn Report 1977. *The Structure of the Curriculum in the Third and Fourth Years of the Scottish Secondary School*. SED/HMSO

Osborn, V. 1968. 'Teaching language to disadvantaged children' in Brottman, M. (ed.), *Language remediation for the disadvantaged pre-school child*, Monographs of the society for research in child development, 33, No. 8

Rosen, C. & Rosen, H. 1973. *The language of primary school children*. Penguin Education

Trudgill, P. 1975. *Accent, dialect and the school*. Edward Arnold

Suggested further reading

Brown, S. 1980. *What do they know? A review of criterion-referenced assessment*. HMSO

Carter, R. (ed.) 1982. *Linguistics and the teacher*. Routledge & Kegan Paul

Donaldson, M. 1978. *Children's minds*. Fontana

Doughty, P., Pierce, J. & Thornton, G. 1971. *Language in use*. Edward Arnold

Stubbs, M. 1976. *Language, schools and classrooms*. Methuen

Trudgill, P. 1975. *Accent, dialect and the school*. Edward Arnold

Index